D1282049

Editorial Research Reports

ON THE

URBAN
ENVIRONMENT

Published by Congressional Quarterly, Inc.
1735 K Street, N.W.
Washington, D.C. 20006

30/.36
E
c./

12/12/69
Pub

Published January 1969
Library of Congress Catalogue Card Number 69-18732

Editorial Research Reports
Editor Emeritus, Richard M. Boeckel
Editor, William B. Dickinson, Jr.

Contents

FOREWORD

CITIES have been described as the new frontiers of 20th century America, full of the promise and the peril of the old frontiers. As America enters the final year of this decade, the emphasis is on the dangers of city life, not its virtues. Crime in the streets, pollution in the air, crowding and exploitation in the slums, unresponsive local government, mindless architectural planning—these are a few of the irritations that erode the quality of city living and throw a shadow over the fearful suburbs.

Looking at an urban landscape beset by garbage, smog, junk, and sewage, author George R. Stewart was moved to comment: "The American world gives some indication of ending in a bad smell." That there is in fact a real emergency does seem to be impressing itself at last on the public consciousness, if not its conscience. Stirrings in the Congress and in the state legislatures give hope that the nation is ready to turn its energies inward to the task of saving the urban environment from a final crisis.

One of the reasons for the tardy response has been the lack of public awareness that America has undergone a revolution in its living habits. Only 5 per cent of the nation's inhabitants were urban dwellers when the first census was taken in 1790. The country remained predominantly rural until the second decade of the 20th century. But today two out of every three Americans live in one of the nation's 219 metropolitan areas. Unfortunately, nostalgia for a vanished past threatens to delay reforms necessary to meet the changed conditions. The malaise is not restricted to the United States. Greek city planner Constantinos Doxiadis warns that "all big cities of mankind are sliding into chaos."

The nine Editorial Research Reports published in this volume reflect a few of the challenges that must be faced—now—if city dwellers are to avoid dropping deeper into the behavioral sink. It should be clear that only a nuclear war could disperse the population back into the countryside. At best the "new town" concept of planning can only slow down the accumulation of people and grievances in our megalopolises. Americans either will learn to live in their melting pot environment or perish in it. The domestic headlines of the day mirror the frightening fact that the decision hangs in the balance.

William B. Dickinson, Jr.
Editor

January 1969
Washington, D.C.

POPULATION PROFILE OF THE UNITED STATES

by

Helen B. Shaffer

1 9 6 7
Nov. 1

POPULATION PROFILE
OF THE UNITED STATES

AT ELEVEN O'CLOCK on the morning of November 20, 1967, the Census Clock in Washington, D. C., will tick off the arrival of the 200 millionth inhabitant of the United States.[1] Exactly 14½ seconds later, the clock will move on to show a total population of 200,000,001. At the current rate of population growth, as estimated by the Bureau of the Census, approximately 250 persons are added to the population every hour.

Actually, the 200-million mark probably was reached many months ago. The official count is known to miss a number of floaters in the population; the census takers themselves estimate they overlooked 5.7 million Americans in 1960.[2] But a difference of a few months or years in the time of passing the 200-million milestone does not alter the significance of the event as a reminder of the inexorable growth of population and the problems it presents for the future.

Until recently, the prospect of overpopulation in the United States seemed remote, if not non-existent. At the start, the country had so sparse a population and so vast a continent on which to expand that its capacity to accommodate more people seemed limitless. A declining birth rate during most of the years of national growth allayed fears of potential overpopulation and even gave rise to concern that economic stagnation might follow a population decline.

Only 30 years ago the cabinet-level National Resources Committee submitted to President Franklin D. Roosevelt a book-length report dealing with the "economic and social problems" attendant on "the change from an expanding to a

---

[1] The Census Clock in the lobby of the Department of Commerce building automatically registers the one-by-one gain in the country's population on the basis of estimates of current birth, death, immigration and emigration rates.

[2] A large share of the persons not counted are thought to have been in the lower strata of urban society. As a result, problems related to indigency in the cities probably are greater than official statistics indicate. See *Congressional Quarterly Weekly Report* of Sept. 8, 1967, pp. 1762-1763.

stabilized or slowly decreasing national population." [3] Most demographers and social planners of the New Deal era foresaw a future of population decline. Their predictions were discredited by the rising birth rate of the 1940s.

Today there are still experts who believe the United States is headed eventually for a halt to population growth. But no one doubts that, barring an unforeseen catastrophe, the population will grow rapidly in the remaining decades of the present century, requiring adjustments in nearly every area of American life. No one is sure what effect sheer numbers will have on the living style and the personal and social aspirations of the American people in the years of change ahead. Clues may be found by reviewing how the population changed during the past years of growth and by examining what the population is like today as the nation sets out to accumulate its third hundred million of inhabitants.

PHENOMENAL GROWTH IN COUNTRY'S EARLY YEARS

Growth of the population of European colonists in the part of the New World that was to become the United States was viewed, even in its own time, as one of the wonders of the world. From 210 souls in 1610, the number grew—largely through immigration—to 85,000 in 1660.[4] After that year, the population increased by about 35 per cent in every decade until 1770 when, on the eve of the American Revolution, there were an estimated 2,205,000 persons of European birth or descent in the 13 colonies.

The most remarkable feature of this phenomenally high growth rate, which more than doubled the population every quarter-century, was that it was due very largely, after 1660, to natural increase. Studies of early records show that in most of the colonies the annual births probably were "twice as numerous as any steady amount of annual net immigration within 10 years after the initial settlements were made." It has been estimated that in 1750, when the total population was approximately 1,207,000, there were 66,000 births and 4,000 immigrants.[5]

---

[3] National Resources Committee, *The Problems of a Changing Population* (May 1938), p. 7. The over-all tone of the report was optimistic, the authors seeking to allay a widely held view at the time that declining population growth had contributed to onset of the Great Depression.

[4] U. S. Census Bureau, *A Century of Population Growth in the United States, 1790-1900* (1909), p. 9.

[5] Donald J. Bogue, *The Population of the United States* (1959), p. 292.

GROWTH OF POPULATION OF THE
UNITED STATES, 1790 - 1967

Census date	Number (thousands)	Per cent increase over preceding census
1790 (Aug. 2)	3,929	......
1800 (Aug. 4)	5,308	35.1
1810 (Aug. 6)	7,240	36.4
1820 (Aug. 7)	9,638	33.1
1830 (June 1)	12,866	33.5
1840 (June 1)	17,069	32.7
1850 (June 1)	23,192	35.9
1860 (June 1)	31,443	35.6
1870 (June 1)	39,818*	26.6
1880 (June 1)	50,156	26.0
1890 (June 1)	62,948	25.5
1900 (June 1)	75,995	20.7
1910 (Apr. 15)	91,972	21.0
1920 (Jan. 1)	105,711	14.9
1930 (Apr. 1)	122,775	16.1
1940 (Apr. 1)	131,669	7.2
1950 (Apr. 1)	150,697	14.5
1960 (Apr. 1)	178,464	18.4
1967 (Apr. 1, est.)	197,430	10.5 (7 years)

* Adjusted for under-enumeration of Southern States.
SOURCES: U. S. Bureau of the Census, *Statistical Abstract of the United States: 1967* (Eightieth edition), Washington, D. C., 1967, p. 5 and *Current Population Reports*, Series P-25, No. 372, Aug. 21, 1967.

The ease with which a new family could acquire good farmland in the colonies, compared with the situation in Europe, encouraged early marriage and a resultant high birth rate. It has been estimated that married women in the colonial and early federal period bore on the average eight children apiece; the average today is three. Historians also find evidence of an appreciable improvement in the death rate, especially among children, over that in the home countries, probably due in large part to the absence of infection-spreading congestion in the colonies.[6] It was no wonder that "in 1790 if not at a much earlier date, the proportion of the population that was American-born was well over 90 per cent." [7]

This extraordinary fecundity continued during the early decades of the Republic, a period of relatively small immigration. Commenting on conditions in the young Republic

[6] Village wells common in Europe at the time were a source of contagious intestinal infection deadly to children, a hazard from which the colonists' children were free.— Warren S. Thompson and David T. Lewis, *Population Problems* (Fifth edition, 1965), pp. 408-410.

[7] Bogue, *op. cit.*, p. 293. Historians' estimates of the numbers who left Europe for North America before the Revolution range from 750,000 to 2,000,000, but there are no statistics on the number who died en route, who landed elsewhere than in the 13 colonies, or who came to the colonies but later returned to the home country.

that were conducive to population growth, a former French consular official wrote in 1814: "No human consideration there operates as a hindrance to reproduction and the children swarm on the rich land in the same manner as do insects." [8]

BIRTH RATE AND IMMIGRATION AS GROWTH FACTORS

The birth rate soon entered on a slow but long-term decline that brought it down from 55 per 1,000 population in 1820 to 18.4 per 1,000 in 1933. But rising immigration, spurred by the development of abundant opportunities in trade, industry and agriculture, helped to offset the effect on population growth of the declining rate of reproduction. A declining death rate also helped. [9] The population thus continued to grow by about one-third between each decennial census until 1860. The rate of increase then began a steady decline, despite heavy immigration up to World War I.

Immigration became an increasingly important source of population increase after 1840. Ten million persons entered the United States between 1840 and 1880, and 22 million arrived during the next 35 years. Heavy immigration was checked after World War I when Congress imposed restrictions that applied with particular severity to the countries that had been supplying the large majority of immigrants.

From peak rates of more than one million a year in the first decade of the century, immigration fell to a wartime low of 110,600 in 1918. Even after the Immigration Acts of 1921 and 1924 were put into effect, the number of arrivals averaged around 300,000 a year. But the number fell to a trickle during the depression of the 1930s and did not regain its six-figure strength until after World War II.

The decline of immigration coincided with a sharp drop in the birth rate. The result was a fall in the rate of population growth to a mere 7 per cent in the decade between the 1930 and 1940 censuses. It was at this point that demographers and other authorities spoke gloomily of "the deficit in our vital account" and the threat of "population decline

---

[8] Chevalier Felix de Beaujour, *Sketch of the United States of North America* (1814), quoted by Bogue, *op. cit.*, p. 291.

[9] Reliable death statistics before 1900 are scarce, but it is generally accepted that the great medical discoveries of the 19th century brought down the death rate. The crude death rate in 1800 has been estimated at 25-28 per 1,000 population (Bogue, *op. cit.*, p. 168). In 1900 it was 17.2 per 1,000; the 1966 rate was 9.5.

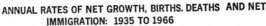

ANNUAL RATES OF NET GROWTH, BIRTHS. DEATHS AND NET
IMMIGRATION: 1935 TO 1966

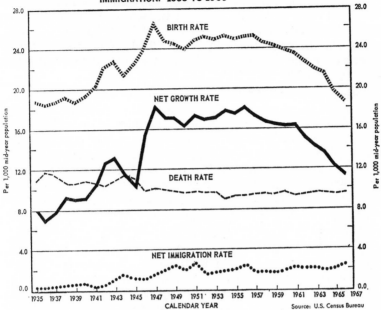

and ultimate extinction of certain stocks" if the trend continued.[10]

BABY BOOM AND POPULATION TRENDS SINCE 1945

The baby boom of the 1940s and 1950s—dramatic as it was in reversing the low fertility level of the 1930s—obscured the fact that the long-term decline in the birth rate that began a century and a half earlier was continuing. The boom years now appear on the birth rate chart as a brief upward interlude on a long descending curve rather than as a rise to a higher plateau. In most of the depression years, the birth rate fluctuated between 18 and 19 per 1,000 population, reaching bottom at 18.4 in 1933 and 1936. The rate began to climb in 1940.

A salient fact about the baby boom is that the birth rate, even at its postwar peak (26.6 in 1947) was still lower than it was in 1920 (27.7) and much lower than it was in 1915 (29.5) or 1910 (30.1) or 1900 (32.3). Even more striking is the fact that the decline since 1957 (when the rate was 25.2) has brought the current rate down to 18.6 (in 1966), almost the lowest in American history.

---

[10] Louis I. Dublin, "Introduction," and Alfred J. Lotka, "Modern Trends in the Birth Rate," *Annals of the American Academy of Political and Social Science,* November 1936, pp. x and 6.

The result has been a decline in the pace of annual population growth from 1.83 per cent in 1956 to 1.15 per cent in 1966. The 3,661,000 babies born in 1966 were 140,000 fewer than the number born in 1965 (3,801,000) and 671,000 fewer than the number born in the year of the biggest baby crop (4,332,000 in 1957).

Other factors considered in computing the growth rate have become negligible. The death rate appears to have stabilized over the past decade at around 9.5 per 1,000 population. Net immigration has become a minor factor. The Immigration Act of 1965 and the U.S.-Cuba agreement of the same year on refugees [11] accounted for an increase from the 300,000-400,000 levels of the previous 15 years to 456,000 in 1966. But even this relatively high figure is only two-tenths of one per cent of the total population.

Despite the slowing pace of growth, the numerical increase of population has been large and promises to become larger as more girls born in the baby boom period reach child-bearing years. From 132 million Americans in 1940, just before the birth rate shot up, the population rose to 198,110,000 on Jan. 1, 1967: a 50 per cent gain in a quarter-century. It took the nation two and one-half centuries to gain its first 100 million people (in 1915) but little more than half a century to raise the total to 200 million.

Patterns of Change in the Population

AS THE POPULATION of the United States grew, its components changed. The people spread in new patterns over an expanding land area. Age groupings and ethnic composition changed, and the changes were themselves important factors affecting growth.

From the beginning, the American population was characterized by movement—immigration from other lands and considerable migration within national borders. Pushing back of the frontier inevitably drew population westward, but even after 1890, when most of the good land had been

---

[11] The Immigration Act of 1965 established annual quotas of 120,000 from the Western Hemisphere, 170,000 from other parts of the world, and an estimated 30,000-40,000 near-relatives of U.S. citizens. The U.S.-Cuba agreement provided for admission to the United States of Cubans who wished to leave their country to join members of their families, or to leave for other acceptable reasons.

Regional Distribution of the Population of the U.S. 1940 to 1985

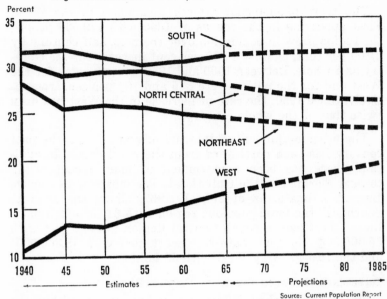

Percent

35

30

25

20

15

10

1940　45　50　55　60　65　70　75　80　1985

SOUTH

NORTH CENTRAL

NORTHEAST

WEST

Estimates ──────── Projections ────

Source: Current Population Report

taken up, the West continued to exert a pull on population. Not even the depression of the 1930s could stop it entirely.[12]

When the first census was taken in 1790, fewer than one of every 20 Americans lived west of the Appalachian Mountains. Ninety years later, one-half of the country's inhabitants lived on land that had become a part of the United States since 1790.

The population of 4 million in 1790 was equally divided between North (today's Northeast) and South, and those two regions grew at an even pace for much of the nation's history. But the North Central region, which first appeared in the census of 1800 with a population of 51,000, grew faster than either of the two older sections and overtook them in population count by 1870.[13]

[12] John Steinbeck's novel *Grapes of Wrath* (1939) dramatized the migration in the 1930s of poor farmers from the dustbowl states to the fertile valleys of California.

[13] The states are now divided as follows into four standard census regions:

Northeast. Connecticut, Massachusetts, Maine, New Hampshire, New Jersey, New York, Pennsylvania, Rhode Island, Vermont.

North Central. Illinois, Indiana, Iowa, Kansas, Michigan, Minnesota, Missouri, Nebraska, North Dakota, Ohio, South Dakota, Wisconsin.

South. Alabama, Arkansas, Delaware, District of Columbia, Florida, Georgia, Kentucky, Louisiana, Maryland, Mississippi, North Carolina, Oklahoma, South Carolina, Tennessee, Texas, Virginia, West Virginia.

West. Alaska, Arizona, California, Colorado, Hawaii, Idaho, Montana, Nevada, New Mexico, Oregon, Utah, Washington, Wyoming.

9

The truly phenomenal growth took place in the West. First appearing in the census of 1850 with 179,000 people, the region grew in population over the next half century by 2,200 per cent, against a 230 per cent increase for the country as a whole. Between 1900 and 1950, growth rates for the West and for the nation were 375 and 100 per cent, respectively. Since 1950, the rate of increase in the West has been twice that of the whole country.

The other major pull of internal migration over the past century has been northward from the rural South. In addition, there has been a movement of more recent origin toward Florida and the Gulf Coast. The most recent Census Bureau estimate, as of July 1, 1967, shows the 16-state South still the most populous region with 61,500,000 inhabitants; the 12-state North Central Region next largest with 55,000,000; the nine-state Northeast next with 48,300,000; and the fast-growing West with 33 million.

DIFFERENCES BETWEEN STATES IN GROWTH RATES

There are marked differences among states within the regions. In the decade 1950-60, for example, the annual rate of growth among states in the West ranged from 5.6 per cent in Alaska and 5.5 per cent in Arizona to 1.2 per cent in Idaho (annual rate for the nation: 1.7 per cent). Among the 16 states of the South, Arkansas and West Virginia each lost 0.7 per cent, while Florida had the fastest annual growth rate in the country—5.8 per cent. Between 1960 and July 1, 1967, five states lost population, and the increase among the others ranged from less than 1 per cent in Maine to 57 per cent in Nevada.

No other state has had so phenomenal and long-lasting a growth as California. From an estimated non-Indian population of 14,000 in 1848, the year gold was discovered, the number jumped to 93,000 in 1850, the year California became a state. Over the next half-century, the population of California increased nearly 1,400 per cent; Vermont, by comparison, experienced only a 9 per cent growth in the same interval. California entered the Union ranking 31st in population; the 1960 census showed it in second place, and by 1965 it had overtaken New York. The most recent estimate (July 1967) gives California 19.2 million people and New York 18.3 million.[14]

---

[14] New York had been the No. 1 state in population since 1810 when it displaced Virginia at the summit.

1967 POPULATION ESTIMATES

State	1940 Population	1960 Population	July 1, 1967 Population	1940-1967 Percent Change
Alabama	2,833,000	3,267,000	3,540,000	+ 24.9%
Alaska	73,000	226,000	273,000	+273.9
Arizona	499,000	1,302,000	1,635,000	+227.7
Arkansas	1,949,000	1,786,000	1,969,000	+ 1.0
California	6,907,000	15,717,000	19,163,000	+177.4
Colorado	1,123,000	1,754,000	1,975,000	+ 75.9
Connecticut	1,709,000	2,535,000	2,925,000	+ 71.2
Delaware	267,000	446,000	523,000	+ 95.9
Florida	1,897,000	4,952,000	5,996,000	+216.1
Georgia	3,124,000	3,943,000	4,511,000	+ 44.4
Hawaii	423,000	633,000	741,000	+ 75.2
Idaho	525,000	667,000	699,000	+ 33.1
Illinois	7,897,000	10,081,000	10,894,000	+ 38.0
Indiana	3,428,000	4,662,000	4,999,000	+ 45.8
Iowa	2,538,000	2,758,000	2,753,000	+ 8.5
Kansas	1,801,000	2,179,000	2,275,000	+ 26.3
Kentucky	2,846,000	3,038,000	3,191,000	+ 12.1
Louisiana	2,364,000	3,257,000	3,660,000	+ 54.8
Maine	847,000	969,000	973,000	+ 14.9
Maryland	1,821,000	3,101,000	3,685,000	+102.4
Massachusetts	4,317,000	5,149,000	5,421,000	+ 25.6
Michigan	5,256,000	7,823,000	8,584,000	+ 63.3
Minnesota	2,792,000	3,414,000	3,582,000	+ 28.3
Mississippi	2,184,000	2,178,000	2,348,000	+ 7.5
Missouri	3,785,000	4,320,000	4,605,000	+ 21.7
Montana	559,000	675,000	701,000	+ 25.4
Nebraska	1,316,000	1,411,000	1,435,000	+ 9.0
Nevada	110,000	285,000	444,000	+303.6
New Hampshire	492,000	607,000	685,000	+ 39.2
New Jersey	4,160,000	6,067,000	7,004,000	+ 68.4
New Mexico	532,000	951,000	1,003,000	+ 88.5
New York	13,479,000	16,782,000	18,335,000	+ 36.0
North Carolina	3,572,000	4,556,000	5,027,000	+ 40.7
North Dakota	642,000	632,000	639,000	− .5
Ohio	6,908,000	9,706,000	10,462,000	+ 51.4
Oklahoma	2,336,000	2,328,000	2,496,000	+ 6.9
Oregon	1,090,000	1,769,000	1,999,000	+ 83.4
Pennsylvania	9,900,000	11,319,000	11,626,000	+ 17.4
Rhode Island	713,000	859,000	901,000	+ 26.4
South Carolina	1,900,000	2,383,000	2,603,000	+ 37.0
South Dakota	643,000	681,000	674,000	+ 4.8
Tennessee	2,916,000	3,567,000	3,888,000	+ 33.3
Texas	6,415,000	9,580,000	10,873,000	+ 69.5
Utah	550,000	891,000	1,022,000	+ 85.8
Vermont	359,000	390,000	416,000	+ 15.9
Virginia	2,678,000	3,967,000	4,533,000	+ 69.3
Washington	1,736,000	2,853,000	3,089,000	+ 77.9
West Virginia	1,902,000	1,860,000	1,798,000	− 5.5
Wisconsin	3,138,000	3,952,000	4,188,000	+ 33.5
Wyoming	251,000	330,000	315,000	+ 25.5
District of Columbia	663,000	764,000	809,000	+ 22.0
TOTALS	132,165,000	179,323,000	197,884,000	+ 49.7

Florida's rapid growth began later than California's, but it has been almost as extraordinary. Between 1900 and 1950 the population of Florida grew more than four times as fast as that of the country as a whole. Recent Census Bureau figures show it growing at double the national rate. Though 22d in the country in land area, Florida now ranks eighth in population. Among the 16 states of the South, it is second only to Texas, which is five times as large.

URBANIZATION AND SPREAD OF METROPOLITAN AREAS

Only 5 per cent of the nation's inhabitants were urban dwellers when the first census was taken; there were then 24 urban places (at least 2,500 population), New York being the largest with a population of 33,000. The country remained predominantly rural until the second decade of the 20th century. The 1920 census was first to tip the balance with 51.2 per cent counted as city dwellers. From 1810 on (except in the decade 1870-80) the rate of increase of the rural population had declined, but not until 1960 did the census show a decline in the actual number of rural dwellers. However, the 54 million rural dwellers in that year constituted only 30 per cent of the population.

Departure from the farm accounts largely for the drop in the proportion of the rural to the whole population. On the eve of World War I, one-third of the people still lived on farms; today only one in 17 does. The farm population in 1966 was estimated at 11.6 million, down from 15.6 million in 1960. The current rate of farm population loss—about 5 per cent a year—is expected to continue.

The age and sex distribution of the farm population has shown radical changes. In the past, the child population was higher on the farm than in the city. But the tendency of farmers' children to leave when they reach maturity has resulted in a sharp lowering of the birth rate on the farm. The relatively high rate of out-migration by rural Negroes, who tended to have a higher birth rate than white farm families, also has depressed population growth in rural areas.

The drift of farm dwellers to the city and the tendency of immigrants from abroad to settle in the more populous centers led to a growth of town and city that took the form of what has become known as the metropolitan area. Ever since metropolitan areas were first reported in the 1910 census, their rate of population growth has far exceeded that for the country as a whole.

CHANGE IN POPULATION DENSITY
OF UNITED STATES SINCE 1790

Census date	Land area in square miles	Population	Persons per square mile of land area
CONTERMINOUS U.S.[1]			
1790	864,746	3,929,214	4.5
1800	864,746	5,308,483	6.1
1810	1,681,828	7,239,881	4.3
1820	1,749,462	9,638,453	5.5
1830	1,749,462	12,866,020	7.4
1840	1,749,462	17,069,453	9.8
1850	2,940,042	23,191,876	7.9
1860	2,969,640	31,443,321	10.6
1870	2,969,640	39,818,449	13.4
1880	2,969,640	50,155,783	16.9
1890	2,969,640	62,947,714	21.2
1900	2,969,834	75,994,575	25.6
1910	2,969,565	91,972,266	31.0
1920	2,969,451	105,710,620	35.6
1930	2,977,128	122,775,046	41.2
1940	2,977,128	131,669,275	44.2
1950	2,974,726	150,697,361	50.7
1960	2,971,494	178,464,236	60.1
UNITED STATES			
1950	3,552,206	151,325,798	42.6
1960	3,548,974	179,323,175	50.5

[1] Excludes Alaska and Hawaii.

A Census Bureau report showed that on July 1, 1965, there were 219 metropolitan areas with a combined population constituting two-thirds of the total population. "Metropolitanization of the population of the United States appears to be continuing but apparently at a somewhat reduced pace in the first half of the 1960 decade as compared with the 1950s." [15]

The fastest growing metropolitan area of the 1960s has been Las Vegas, Nev., which added 80 per cent to its population in 5½ years. The Oxnard-Ventura and Anaheim-Santa Ana-Garden Grove, Calif., metropolitan areas both experienced increases well over 50 per cent, mostly in the form of suburban spillover from Los Angeles County. Forty-five per cent increases were reported in Huntsville, Ala., site of missile research, and in Santa Barbara, Calif. Ten other metropolitan areas showed increases of more than 25 per cent in the half-decade. The largest numerical increase occurred in the Los Angeles-Long Beach metropolitan area, which added more than 700,000 people. The New York

[15] Population living in metropolitan area counties grew 60 per cent faster than population elsewhere in the country during the 1960-65 period, but it grew nearly five times as fast in the 1950-60 decade, according to a U. S. Census Bureau report of Aug. 14, 1967.

metropolitan area added 650,000, while the Chicago and Washington areas each gained more than 400,000. A total of 28 metropolitan areas added more than 100,000 to their populations in the half-decade.

The result is higher density of population in some areas, and sparse population in many others. The country began with a population density of 4.5 persons per square mile over its 864,700 square-mile land area. The figure rose to a little over 50 per square mile in 1960, about double the density of 1910. But the national figure tells little of the actual crowding where most of the people live. It has been estimated that 56 per cent of the people in conterminous United States (exclusive of Alaska and Hawaii) live on 7 per cent of the land area.[16]

These figures are particularly striking in view of the trend toward extending the geographic area of the metropolitan district by converting rural border land to suburban or satellite-town development. The metropolitan area population growth of recent years has been largely beyond the city proper. The growth rate for central cities in the 1960-66 period (2.8 per cent) was actually lower than the growth rate in non-metropolitan areas (4.2 per cent). Some of the larger cities suffered a slight decline of population.

CHANGES IN AGE DISTRIBUTION AND DEPENDENCY RATIO

Next to urbanization, the most significant changes in the population of the United States have occurred in age distribution. Urbanization and age patterns both have great bearing on past and potential population growth. The recent decline in the birth rate, for example, can be attributed in part to a decrease in the proportion of the population in the fertile years—itself a consequence of the low birth rate of the 1930s and early 1940s.[17]

When the Republic was founded, half of all Americans were under the age of 16. The declining birth rate and the increase in longevity gradually aged the population. By 1950 the average American was past 30. Because of the baby boom, the median age fell to 27.8 in 1966.

Shifts in age patterns affect the size of the burden of

---

[16] "The Continuing Challenge," *Urban Land* (official publication of Urban Land Institute, February 1967), p. 2.

[17] Women in the child-bearing years (15-44) constituted 20 per cent of the population in 1965, compared with 23.9 per cent in 1932. " 'Boom Babies' Come of Age," *Population Bulletin* (Population Reference Bureau, Inc., August 1966), p. 64.

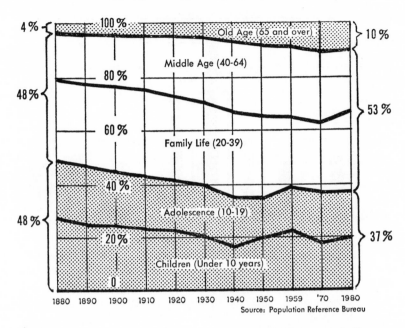

Source: Population Reference Bureau

supporting non-productive segments of the population—primarily the very young and the very old. Until 1940, the "dependency ratio"—the number in the non-producing ages relative to the number in the working ages—had been declining. Immigration in its heaviest years consisted largely of young adult males and thus intensified this trend.[18] In 1820, for each 100 persons of working age (20-64) there were 153 dependents (146 under 20 and 7 over 64). By 1900 the ratio had fallen to 94 (86 young, 8 old). By 1940 it was 71 (59 young, 12 old).[19] Then the ratio began to move in the other direction; in 1965 there were 95 in dependency ages (77 young, 18 old) for every 100 aged 20-64.

CHARACTERISTICS OF NEGRO SEGMENT OF POPULATION

Through migration and natural increase, the Negro has contributed significantly to metropolitan growth. Exodus of Negroes from the rural South and their concentration in the central cities have been familiar elements of the drama of race relations in the United States over the past few decades.

[18] "From the earliest records through the 80s of the 19th century, two-thirds of all immigrants were in the central productive ages from 15 to 39. . . . In the years from 1899 through 1914 more than four-fifths of all immigrants were between the ages of 14 and 44."—Conrad and Irene B. Taeuber, *The Changing Population of the United States* (1958), p. 67.

[19] Philip M. Hauser, *Population Perspectives* (1960), p. 70.

Change in White and Nonwhite Population by Age: 1960 to 1965

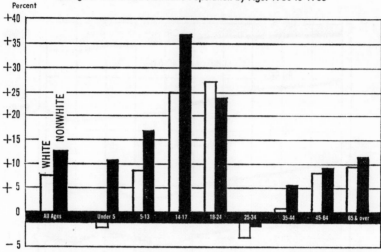

Source: U.S. Census Bureau

This movement of Negro population is continuing. Of the 2.9 million rise in total nonwhite population between 1960 and mid-1966, 2.5 million was in the central cities of metropolitan areas. The extent to which the increase occurred in the central cities was even more marked than in the 1950-60 decade, the Census Bureau reported. As a result, 55 per cent of the nonwhite population is now living in the central cities.

The proportion of Negroes in the population decreased steadily from an estimated 19 per cent in 1790 to a low of 9.7 per cent in 1930. Since then, the proportion has been rising, reaching 10.5 per cent in 1960 and an estimated 11 per cent as of July 1, 1966. The relatively high birth rate— 26.5 per 1,000 of the Negro population in 1966 against 17.5 for the white population—and the relative youth of the Negro population suggest that a rapid increase may be expected in the years immediately ahead. The number of white children under five was 4.2 per cent smaller in 1966 than in 1960. Though the Negro as well as the white birth rate declined, it was still sufficiently high to account for a 7.6 per cent increase in the number of Negro children under five.

Over the same period, the Negro population aged 5-13 rose 19.8 per cent, and that aged 14-17 rose 40.6 per cent. Increases for the white population in those age groups amounted to 10.2 and 26.3 per cent, respectively. Census Bureau projections for future population growth indicate a

16

rise of Negro population to around 14-15 per cent of the total population by 1990. Census estimates as of July 1, 1966, showed 21.6 million Negroes, 2 million other non-whites, and 173.2 million whites in the population.

Population Growth in the Years Ahead

WHAT of the future? Demographers rarely make predictions any more. Too many earlier forecasts have been proved far out of line. The word today is "projection." The size of the population at a future date is calculated on the basis of certain assumptions about the continuation or modification of current trends in birth, death, and migration rates. The Census Bureau has projected four sets of future growth figures based on an estimated population of 196,842,000 on July 1, 1966. Differences among the four are due chiefly to differences in assumptions about future fertility rates.

The lowest of the four projections for 1985 places the total population in that year at 241,731,000, the highest at 274,748,000. The former projection indicates that the population will reach 300 million at some time between 2005 and 2010. Under the highest projection, a total of 300 million would be reached by 1990 and a total of 400 million between 2005 and 2010.

PREFERENCES OF COUPLES AS TO SIZE OF FAMILIES

The future of population growth rests on what Robert C. Cook, president of the Population Reference Bureau, has referred to as "a multitude of individual decisions"—that is, the decisions made by young married couples on the number of children they want to have. "The attitudes of these young marrieds toward family planning," said Cook, "are crucial as a major determinant of social and economic growth of this nation." [20]

Advent of the contraceptive pill has been widely regarded as foreshadowing still lower fertility rates. Yet long before the pill became available, most couples had a high degree of success in regulating the number of births in their families. A high birth rate has been associated historically with low economic and educational status. A lowering of the birth

---

[20] "'Boom Babies' Come of Age," *Population Bulletin* (Population Reference Bureau, Inc., August 1966), p. 62.

rate is therefore expected when the population as a whole attains a higher level of prosperity. The Industrialization and urbanization also have been viewed as family-limiting factors, while life on a farm has been considered conducive to the breeding of large families.

Trends of recent years, however, have not always reflected these general principles. It is true that the birth rate is relatively high among the poor, but many of the high-breeding poor are in the cities, not the country. And the sharp rise in the birth rate in the 1940s and 1950s resulted not from ignorance, poverty, the influences of rural living, or even the conditions of war and its aftermath, but primarily from the desire of large numbers of young people to marry early and to have more children than their parents did.

Family plans of couples in the years immediately ahead are of particular moment because those born in the baby-boom years are now reaching their fertile years. According to Dr. Arthur A. Campbell of the Vital Statistics Division of the U. S. Public Health Service, the number of women of child-bearing age will be 26 per cent greater in 1970 than in 1965.[21] And Robert Cook of the Population Reference Bureau has pointed out that the number of women in the most fertile years of all—20-29—will rise from 14 million in 1967 to 20 million in 1980. A tendency to marry early is now apparently well entrenched. The prospect therefore is for a marked population increase even if there is no increase in the average number of children per family.

The fertility rate—that is, the number of births per 1,000 women in the 15-44 age bracket—ranged between 76 and 79 during the depression. If it had continued at that level, the population in 1960 would have been somewhere between 130 million and 150 million instead of 180 million. Actually, the fertility rate rose to 123 in 1957, then slipped down to 91.8 in 1966. "That the nation is balanced on a demographic hair trigger," commented Cook, "is shown by the fact that . . . if the women of the United States were to average four children instead of three, by the year 2000 the population increase would exceed the present population."

There are some indications of a growing preference for a slightly smaller family than was desired a decade ago. The

---

[21] Conference on population problems, New York, April 14, 1967.

Population Projection to 1990

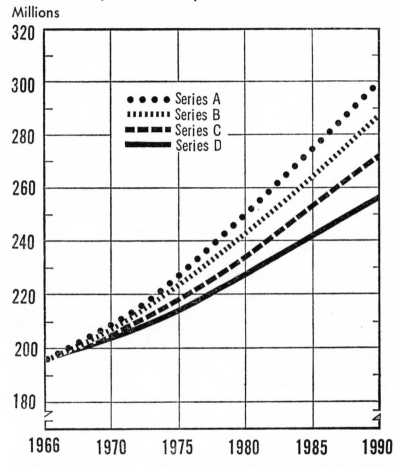

Millions

Source: Statistical Abstract of the U.S. 1967

National Center for Health Statistics of the U. S. Public Health Service reported earlier this year that there had been a drop in the birth rate among wives over 30, and that younger couples appeared to be spacing births more widely than in the past. A study based on the results of a survey in 1960 by the Princeton Office of Population Research showed that an overwhelming majority of married women considered two, three, or four children the ideal number; four was the most popular choice. But some significance was seen in the finding that the youngest wives—aged 18-24—expected the smallest families. Barring major catastrophe, it would require an average of 2.1 children per woman to maintain the population at its present size.

IMPORTANCE OF STABILIZING GROWTH OF POPULATION

Demographers have warned of the consequences of undue population growth in the United States. "There is no danger in this nation for some time to come of being unable to feed our growing population or even of being unable to continue to increase our level of living as measured by income per capita," Dr. Philip M. Hauser, director of the Population Research and Training Center at the University of Chicago, testified last year at a Senate hearing on the "population crisis." [22] But Dr. Hauser foresaw "great danger that the quality of American life . . . may be further diminished." The nation was already "paying a high price" for the postwar baby boom, he said, citing school overcrowding and deterioration, juvenile delinquency and crime, unemployment of youths, exacerbation of race tensions, traffic accidents, and increased air and water pollution.

Roger Revelle, director of the Center for Population Studies at Harvard University, is another who has urged more public awareness of the social and economic costs of rising numbers in the United States. He too has stressed the "decline in the quality of life," and the "increase in per capita costs of pollution abatement, municipal water supplies, outdoor recreation, and urban transportation."

Many of the problems cited as a consequence of population growth result largely from the clustering of people in urban areas. A major study of metropolitan growth, conducted by the Urban Land Institute under a Ford Foundation grant, foresees an eventual consolidation of the country's population within three great urban regions.

The Atlantic Seaboard Urban Area, which now extends from Augusta, Maine, to Prince William County, Va., was projected to the year 2000 with a one-third increase in land area and a doubling of population, resulting in a population density of 1,050 persons per square mile. The three major metropolises of Florida (Miami, Tampa-St. Petersburg, Jacksonville) would become a continuous urban region with a density of 682 persons per square mile (1,050 on the Florida East Coast). The California "megalopolis" would

[22] Senate Committee on Government Operations, Subcommittee on Foreign Aid Expenditures, Jan. 26, 1966.

link Oakland-San Francisco with Los Angeles for a population growth from 13.8 million to 44.5 million, producing a population density of 923 persons per square mile (1,220 in southern California).

Jerome P. Pickard, research director of the Urban Land Institute, saw benefits in such a development because it would keep the population density relatively low in large parts of the country. "This 'great reserve of space,' " he wrote, "undoubtedly will be in great demand for all forms of recreation and other uses, including food production for the immense population of the urbanized regions." [23] But the Population Reference Bureau has asserted that California as it is today should demonstrate to the remainder of the country the gravity of "political, social, and economic problems . . . intensified by this fantastic proliferation of people." The state's first need, the bureau said, is "simple, clear irrefutable recognition that the growth of California's population must be checked." [24]

How to win voluntary support for population growth limitation is a question yet to be tackled. A Californian concerned with the problems of his state has suggested that it discourage population growth by cutting off the provision of facilities for expansion. Specifically, it should stop developing more water resources, stop building additional power stations and freeways, and stop inviting new industries to come into the state—even if such drastic action does go "against the entire philosophy of the expanding economy." [25]

American business, which is already looking forward to the growth of "new households"—that is, the young married couples whose numbers will increase in the years immediately ahead—is not likely to look favorably on measures to promote population stabilization. There are economists, however, who argue that population stabilization would be an economic boon. Dr. Joseph J. Spengler of the Duke University Department of Economics, is among those who believe a decline in the rate of population growth "could somewhat accelerate the rate at which per capita income rises and thus accentuate trends associated with income growth." With higher per capita income, the demand for

---

[23] Jerome P. Pickard, "Future Growth of Major U. S. Urban Regions," *Urban Land*, February 1967, p. 3.

[24] "California: After 19 Million, What?" *Population Bulletin*, June 1966, p. 53.

[25] Raymond F. Dasmann, *The Destruction of California* (1965).

goods and services, especially for "leisure-oriented output," would expand. "The economy will really become opulent, and much of the population affluent." [26]

The public is likely to be more impressed by the argument that a stabilized population would reduce demands for costly public services. A small foretaste of such a benefit will come as the enrollments in elementary school stop bounding ahead each year as they have been doing for the past eight years. Elementary school enrollments are expected to remain fairly level for the next few years and may even decline in the 1970s. As the years pass, the reduction of pressure should move up from elementary schools to high schools and to colleges. The relatively low birth rate of the past few years may thus give the educational establishment a brief respite until the next baby boom comes along.

[26] J. J. Spengler, "Implications of Population Changes for Business" (Address before National Industrial Conference Board, New York City), *Commercial and Financial Chronicle*, Aug. 11, 1966, reprint, p. 4.

MEGALOPOLIS:
PROMISE AND PROBLEMS

by

Jeanne Kuebler

1 9 6 5
Feb. 10

MEGALOPOLIS: PROMISE AND PROBLEMS

MUSHROOMING CITIES and their even more rapidly growing suburbs are raising a major domestic problem for the United States. Intensification of long-standing urban ills—particularly those having to do with land use, transportation and social and physical environment—seems to have outrun the capacity of cities to handle the problems. Meanwhile, a mounting proportion of the country's population is crowding into metropolitan areas to reap the economic, social and intellectual benefits they offer.

President Johnson said in his State of the Union message to Congress, Jan. 4, that the first step in dealing with the problems of urban communities was "to break old patterns —to begin to think, work and plan for the development of entire metropolitan areas." He called for establishment of a new Department of Housing and Urban Development to give assistance in developing "unified long-range policies for metropolitan areas."

The President outlined also a "beautification" program that would involve a "massive effort to save the countryside." He envisioned more parks of all sizes, more public seashores, and more open space; "imaginative programs" to landscape streets and open areas; and landscaping of highways, with provision for more roadside recreation areas. Johnson indicated, in addition, that he would request funds to study high-speed rail transportation between urban centers. Test projects for much faster passenger service between Boston and Washington, traversing the most highly urbanized large region in the world, would be scheduled first, but the benefits of rail travel at 100-plus miles an hour would eventually be extended to other sections of the country.

The programs outlined by the President are not new. Many of them have been proposed before by officials concerned about haphazard growth in densely populated regions. But the problems of urban areas become more pressing as cities and suburbs continue to draw people from rural areas and from depressed industrial regions. The country's urban population [1] rose from 97 million, or 64 per cent of the total, in 1950 to 125 million, or almost 70 per cent of the total, in 1960. In rural areas the non-farm population increased by nine million, while farm population fell sharply; in 1960, non-farm residents of rural areas outnumbered persons living on farms, 40.6 million to 13.5 million.

DIRECTION OF URBAN GROWTH IN UNITED STATES

A large proportion of the urban growth in the decade of the '50s occurred in the suburbs and satellite cities surrounding the great metropolises—New York, Chicago, Los Angeles, Philadelphia and Detroit. These areas are no longer cities but extensive urban complexes, and some of the urban complexes have started to grow together to form gigantic urban regions. A unique region of the latter sort is the great urban belt extending along the Atlantic seaboard from north of Boston to the Virginia counties of suburban Washington. Jean Gottmann, geographer and sociologist, has labeled this region "Megalopolis." [2] Gottmann, in a study for the Twentieth Century Fund, described it as "an almost continuous stretch of urban and suburban areas from southern New Hampshire to northern Virginia and from the Atlantic shore to the Appalachian foothills."

> No other section of the United States has such a large concentration of population, with such a high average density, spread over such a large area. And no other section has a comparable role within the nation or a comparable importance in the world. Here has been developed a kind of supremacy, in politics, in economics, and possibly even in cultural activities, seldom before attained by an area of this size.[3]

More than 38 million people live in Megalopolis; it contains five of the 15 largest cities in the United States: Boston, New York, Philadelphia, Baltimore and Washington. But Megalopolis is not a nightmare extension of Times Square. The region is not only the financial, business, and

---

[1] The urban population includes, generally speaking, all persons living in places having 2,500 or more inhabitants.

[2] The ancient Greeks planned a new city-state which they hoped would become the largest of Greek cities and named it Megalopolis. Webster defines the word as "a very large city" and as "a thickly populated region centering around a metropolis," but Gottmann believes that it can properly be applied in a new sense to the "unique cluster of metropolitan areas of the northeastern seaboard of the United States."

[3] Jean Gottmann, *Megalopolis: The Urbanized Northeastern Seaboard of the United States* (1961), p. 3.

governmental hub of the nation; it is also a large manufacturing region, and it produces substantial quantities of agricultural products. The population of Megalopolis is, on the average, the richest, best educated, best housed and best serviced group of its size in the world. The area's boundaries are expected, in time, to push up into Maine and reach down into southern Virginia.

Although Megalopolis is unique in size and concentration of population, other urban regions of the United States exhibit similar growth. The population of metropolitan areas [4] has increased from 50 per cent of the country's total in 1920 to 55 per cent in 1940 and 63 per cent in 1960. By the end of the 20th century, metropolitan areas are expected to include 73 per cent of the total population — or 250 million Americans.[5] The Los Angeles-Long Beach region, for example, may increase from fewer than 7 million inhabitants to 17 million.

The Outdoor Recreation Resources Review Commission observed in its summary report to the President and Congress in 1962:

> As cities spill out into suburbs and metropolitan areas are formed, they blend together into a "megalopolis." This interlocking will produce chains of heavily populated, built-up regions, each radiating from a central urban core. Across the country, large belts of populated areas will emerge. In the East, there will be a single urbanized tract extending from Portland, Maine, to Norfolk, Virginia. A midwestern urban complex stretching from Detroit to Cleveland may extend eastward through a chain from Lake Erie along the Mohawk and Hudson Valleys and intersect the Atlantic population belt.[6]

Other large urban regions include the area extending along the southern and western shores of Lake Michigan, connecting Chicago's satellite cities in Indiana with Milwaukee; the cities around San Francisco Bay; the area between Houston and Dallas-Fort Worth; and the eastern coast of Florida, including the burgeoning "moonland" area around Cape Kennedy.

STRONGER VOICE FOR CITIES IN LEGISLATIVE BODIES

Officials and citizens of urban regions are hopeful that the problems of those areas will be given more sympathetic

---

[4] A metropolitan area is the area surrounding, and socially and economically integrated with, a central city of 50,000 or more inhabitants.

[5] Outdoor Recreation Resources Review Commission, *Outdoor Recreation for America* (Report to the President and Congress, January 1962), p. 145.

[6] *Ibid.*, p. 145.

attention in Congress and in state legislatures when those bodies have been reapportioned to comply with recent decisions of the Supreme Court in districting cases. The rulings will gradually correct the long-standing imbalance in allocation of seats between less populous rural areas and the cities—an imbalance which frequently has enabled rural communities to dominate state legislatures and left cities under-represented in the House of Representatives at Washington.[7]

State legislatures in recent years have cleared away some of the obstacles blocking solution of problems of cities and urban areas. The Advisory Commission on Intergovernmental Relations pointed out early in 1964 that "The volume of legislation enacted [by the states in 1963] and the degree of legislative attention directed to problems of the large urban areas exceeded that of any comparable period in the past." [8] State legislative action was "especially noteworthy," the commission said, in "liberalizing annexation laws, extending general authority for interjurisdictional contracting and joint enterprises, providing standards for and generally regulating the creation of new municipal incorporations, and in providing financial aid and regulatory authority to meet urban water and sewage needs." An example was the action of the Massachusetts legislature in creating a metropolitan planning district and a metropolitan area planning council for Boston and 50 nearby communities.

The Johnson administration and many of its supporters on Capitol Hill hope that pro-urban sentiment may be strong enough this year to obtain authorization for creation of the proposed Department of Housing and Urban Development. The President said in his State of the Union message that such a department was needed to spearhead the development of American cities. The proposal was first put forward by President Kennedy in 1961, but floor action was held up then, in part because Kennedy favored appointment of a Negro, Robert C. Weaver, Administrator of the Housing and Home Finance Agency, to head the new department. When the House Rules Committee refused to grant a rule for floor action on the administration bill, Kennedy submitted a reorganization plan to create the new

---

[7] See "Reapportionment Struggle," *E.R.R.*, 1964 Vol. II, pp. 703-706 and 716-720.

[8] Advisory Commission on Intergovernmental Relations, Fifth Annual Report to the President, Jan. 31, 1964, p. 2.

department. Under the Reorganization Act of 1949 the plan would have taken effect automatically within 60 days unless disapproved by simple majority vote in either house of Congress. The House of Representatives killed the plan by a 264-150 vote on Feb. 21, 1962.[9]

GROWING TOGETHER OF CITIES IN THE BRITISH ISLES

Urban problems are not exclusively the concern of the United States; nor are they limited to the industrialized and developed countries of the world. A group of experts in environmental health, meeting under World Health Organization auspices in Geneva last June, concluded that "The tremendous increase in urban population clearly justifies the warning that after the question of keeping world peace, metropolitan planning is probably the most serious single problem faced by man in the second half of the 20th century." In some countries, the W.H.O. group pointed out, virtually the whole of the general population increase is concentrated in great metropolitan areas. The urban millions place a staggering burden on national and municipal authorities because of overcrowding and consequent deterioration of the physical and social environment —all of which contributes to delinquency, crime and disease.

Great Britain faces a problem similar to that of the American Megalopolis in the "conurbation"—or growing together of cities—around London. The problem is aggravated by economic stagnation in some other parts of the British Isles. Slightly more than one-third of Britain's 54 million people live in southeastern England, which occupies only 17 per cent of the country's land area. The population explosion and steady migration from less prosperous regions are expected to add 3.5 million people to the Southeast's population over the next 20 years.

To deal with the London conurbation, Britain in 1946 instituted a program of building "new towns." These self-contained communities are designed to provide jobs and housing in the same general area, thus alleviating the commuter crush between London and its surrounding urban rings. Successful to a point, the new towns have not afforded a full answer. Jobs in central London continue to increase, and for the past five years the number of com-

---

[9] See *Congressional Quarterly Almanac 1962*, pp. 380-384.

muters has grown by an average of 20,000 a year. As *The Economist* pointed out last year, "The population increase in one place, the job increase in another, and the commuting increase between them, are London's problem." [10]

The government on March 19, 1964, announced plans for dealing with the question. The program called for development of three new cities and three new towns in the Southeast, the expansion of 15 towns to accommodate roughly twice their existing population, and a doubling of the expanse of the green belt which had been created around London to prevent the metropolis from spreading endlessly into the countryside. Although seemingly ambitious, the program was criticized as too narrowly conceived and as inadequate to handle the problem. An editorial in the *Town Planning Review* last April pointed out:

> The rest of Britain is bound to see the study as accepting the growth of a prosperous regional city in the Southeast, somewhat on the Boston-New York-Washington pattern. And they have reason. If the town developments proposed actually take place within 20 years, not much save kind words and halfpence may be available to help the North.[11]

John T. James, writing in the *Journal of the Town Planning Institute,* had commented earlier on the similarity of the American Megalopolis and the British Southeast:

> There has been a growing awareness over the past few years that we are moving rapidly into a new form of human settlement pattern, best described as a city region. It is this which makes the true planning unit, though it is never static. Its boundaries are always pushing outwards under population pressure, greater wealth and heightened mobility. Within it, one can see the green belt not simply as a defensive barrier against further growth but as a positive and valuable part of the essential local open space pattern. . . . New towns, as well as old, are here to be seen not as self-contained organisms but as specialist and inter-dependent parts of a highly articulated region. Planned dispersal, as distinct from unplanned diffusion, should preserve the sharp distinction between built up and open ground, thus effecting a marriage of town and country rather than a promiscuous liaison.[12]

Other areas are exhibiting signs of similar growth. But in these two regions the prophecies of early social observers appear to be already coming true. H. G. Wells, in his

---

[10] "South East Soporific," *The Economist*, March 21, 1964, p. 1110.

[11] *Town Planning Review*, April 1964, p. 4.

[12] John T. James, "The Next Fifty Years," *Journal of the Town Planning Institute*, January 1964, p. 8.

Anticipations published in 1901, foresaw that " 'town' and 'city' will be, in truth, terms as obsolete as 'mail coach,' " and he said that "for these new areas that grow out of them we want a term." Oswald Spengler wrote two decades later: "I see long after 2,000 A.D. cities laid out for 10 to 20 million inhabitants spread over enormous areas of countryside . . . and notions of traffic and communication that we should regard as fantastic to the point of madness." [13] Jean Gottmann thought the northeastern Megalopolis might be considered "the cradle of a new order in the organization of inhabited space."

Regional Government Instrumentalities

REGIONAL URBAN PLANNING has come into its own in recent decades as urbanites have attempted to deal with problems related to population density, transportation, and recreation facilities. A Regional Planning Committee was formed for the New York area as early as 1922; its first report, submitted in 1929, covered a 22-county area stretching out in a semi-circle from City Hall. The report anticipated spreading of the area's population over a wide area, with industry, stores and recreation facilities arranged to diminish congestion in the core of the metropolitan complex.

JOB OF PROMOTING INTRA-REGIONAL COOPERATION

The New York group and similar agencies elsewhere face a problem created by the existence of multiple governmental jurisdictions within an area that is essentially a unit. There are about 1,400 different governments in the greater New York region. Megalopolis crosses the boundaries of 10 states and the District of Columbia; the region includes 117 counties and numerous cities. Strong rivalries between states, cities, counties and even townships hamper regional cooperation. Robert C. Wood, a student of metropolitan problems and politics, points out that:

> Throughout this century, people have debated the question of whether or not the American political system could countenance an unbridled laissez-faire economy—whether it did not have to intervene by selective measures to redress the balance of competi-

---

[13] Oswald Spengler, *The Decline of the West* (Alfred A. Knopf edition, 1936), p. 91.

31

tion, at times to preserve it, and at times to guide it. But in the
modern metropolitan region, the question is reversed. The issue
is whether or not a modern economic system, requiring positive
stimulation and selective aid and direction by public authority, can
tolerate an unbridled laissez-faire profusion of governments which
systematically avoid any responsibility for these matters.[14]

Some observers believe that in the super-cities of tomorrow distinctions between city, county, state and federal
responsibilities will be erased. Instead, governmental arrangements will be based on functional requirements and
the type of population served. Some small moves in this
direction have already been made. Connecticut, in 1959,
abolished county governments. The Connecticut Development Commission defines economic planning regions for
the state. If one-half of the municipalities in a region approve, a planning agency, authorized to plan for all municipalities in the region, is established.

Rather than attempting a reorganization of existing government agencies, most urban areas have adopted alternatives to meet specific requirements. Roscoe C. Martin, a
specialist in public administration, has identified three
categories of alternatives: Procedural adaptation, structural adaptation, and regional adjustment. Procedural
adaptation includes intercity cooperation, parallel action,
compacts between cities, transfer of functions, exercise of
extraterritorial jurisdiction (e.g., a 1954 Tennessee law
authorized cities to extend public facilities beyond corporate boundaries), and service contracts. Under service
contracts, small municipalities engage to purchase certain
services—such as waste disposal, library services, etc.—
from other jurisdictions. Los Angeles County, for example,
sells 50 different services to 76 cities.

Structural adaptation includes annexation, consolidation
of several cities, merger of city and county governments,
and establishment of "metro" or metropolitan governments.
Finally, regional programs are devised to meet specific
problems affecting an over-all area — transportation, air
pollution, water supply, or the like.

'METRO' GOVERNMENTS OF MIAMI AND NASHVILLE

To meet difficulties posed by multiple jurisdictions, planners a decade ago urged adoption of metropolitan government, the union of many jurisdictions — city, town and

---

[14] Robert C. Wood, *Metropolis Against Itself* (March 1959), p. 44.

county — under a single government. With a few exceptions, the "metro" idea failed to appeal. The citizens of Dade County, Fla., approved a metro government in 1957 and Nashville, Tenn., and its surrounding Davidson County merged in 1962. There are pronounced differences between those two metropolitan governments.

Daniel R. Grant, economic consultant to the planning commission of Nashville and Davidson County, has pointed out that a single government was established for that area,[15] whereas in Florida's Dade County all of the existing municipal governments were retained; responsibility was divided between area-wide aspects and purely local aspects of urban functions. Dade County has a county manager and a small 13-member executive body; Nashville has an elected mayor and a 40-member executive body.[16]

The move toward "metro" government floundered for a number of reasons, including the opposition of groups who believed it to be a Communist-backed scheme for eliminating local governments.[17] Many officials feared that metro governments would not be as efficient as claimed. They believed that "for many urban services, it is more important that their performance be coordinated with the planning and performance of other functions in the metropolitan area than that they be administered by an area-wide jurisdiction."[18] In cases where restrictions are laid on the central body and where performance of certain services is left to the local jurisdictions, administration and supply of crucial services may be hampered. The Dade County charter, for example, has been revised on several occasions. But the revisions, in the opinion of a local observer, will not enable the county "to cope much more readily with the basic problem of finding the revenue to enable Metro to provide new or better county-wide services and, at the same time, furnish municipal-type services to the hundreds of thousands of residents in the unincorporated areas who demand much and are adamant in their

---

[15] There are two districts in the Nashville-Davidson County government: one for urban services and one for general services.

[16] Daniel R. Grant, "Consolidations Compared," *National Civic Review*, January 1963, pp. 12-13.

[17] Mayor Robert F. Wagner of New York City, at a meeting of the Metropolitan Regional Council representing 37 communities in New York, New Jersey, and Connecticut last April 24, denounced "extremist, anti-metro" groups which oppose "every effort at inter-local government cooperation."

[18] Advisory Commission on Intergovernmental Relations, *Performance of Urban Functions: Local and Areawide* (September 1963), p. 27.

refusal to be incorporated or to pay taxes commensurate with services now received." The critic, Thomas J. Wood of the University of Miami, thinks that the county commission will have to propose some sort of merger of Miami and the unincorporated areas.[19]

Werner Z. Hirsch, director of the Institute of Government and Public Affairs at the University of California at Los Angeles, asserts that "Large-scale metropolitan consolidation has turned out to be an unlikely remedy for metropolitan-area problems." [20]   Hirsch said recently that the important virtues claimed for consolidation, such as economies, improved orderly planning, and equity in financing urban government services, failed of realization.

FEDERAL SUPPORT OF AREA-WIDE URBAN PLANNING

The federal government has encouraged area-wide urban planning for the past decade.   The Housing Act of 1954 authorized grants to state, metropolitan, regional and municipal planning agencies and listed as one of its objectives the promotion of comprehensive area planning.   Federal funds for planning grants were increased in 1961 from $20 million to $75 million, and the federal share was raised from one-half to two-thirds of a project's cost.

In addition, the 1961 legislation authorized $50 million in federal grants to states and localities to pay up to 30 per cent of the cost of land acquisition in and around urban centers.   This authorization was to create open-space areas for recreational, conservation, scenic and historical purposes. The mass transportation loan program, also authorized by the 1961 law, specified that loans would be made only upon determination that the recipient was developing a "comprehensive and coordinated mass transportation system."

The Federal Aid Highway Act of 1962 requires that, beginning July 1, 1965, individual highway projects in a metropolitan area must conform to a comprehensive transportation planning program.   In 1964 the Senate approved a similar requirement for federally aided projects of all kinds, but the bill died in the House.   It would have provided that applications for federal loans or grants from jurisdictions

---

[19] Thomas J. Wood, "Basic Revision in Dade Charter," *National Civic Review*, January 1964, p. 41.

[20] Werner Z. Hirsch, "Administrative and Fiscal Considerations in Urban Development," *Annals of the American Academy of Political and Social Science*, March 1964, p. 60.

within metropolitan areas be accompanied by a report from a locally established planning agency. This requirement, it was felt, would encourage better coordinated local review and contribute to more effective utilization of federal funds.

H.H.F.A. Administrator Weaver proposed on Jan. 13 that a federal representative be assigned to each of the large metropolitan areas to assist them in applying federal programs that affect urban growth. Weaver explained: "A federal urban representative [initially] would simply offer his good offices, working with officials at all levels of government. Later, various incentives might be introduced into the picture, rewards so to speak, for complying with over-all plans and requirements."

The federal program has undoubtedly had an effect on the development of planning agencies, although many regions established area-wide agencies without federal encouragement. A government survey in mid-1963 revealed that 142 of the then total of 212 standard metropolitan statistical areas had some kind of metropolitan planning activity under way.[21] Thirty-eight of the planning agencies were multijurisdictional, covering two or more counties, cities or towns; two-thirds of these agencies served populations in excess of 500,000.

Proposals for Handling Area Problems

THE COMMON CONCEPT of "megalopolis" calls to mind a picture of heavily populated central cities surrounded by extensive stretches of urban sprawl and bound together by ribbons of concrete highways. This concept focuses on two major problems of urbanized regions — transportation, deemed the most vexing problem, and land use with emphasis on preservation of open space. The two problems are intimately related, for as city workers move farther into the countryside, the need for highways to take them to and from the city multiplies. It has been estimated that at least 50 per cent—and possibly as much as 68 per cent—

---

[21] *"National Survey of Metropolitan Planning"* (study prepared by Housing and Home Finance Agency for the Subcommittee on Intergovernmental Relations of the Senate Committee on Government Operations, Dec. 16, 1963), p. 1.

of surface space in downtown Los Angeles is devoted to vehicle movement and storage.[22]

PRESERVATION OF OPEN SPACE IN URBANIZED REGIONS

Progress toward fulfillment of the American dream of every family housed in its own home on its own plot of land has had the indirect effect of gobbling up vast formerly open areas. It has been estimated that urban sprawl consumes land at the rate of a million acres a day. Use of land for suburban dwellings either drives out farm production or limits space needed for recreation. The unplanned development of suburbia, moreover, is apt to result in a "leapfrogging" of land parcels, many of them too small to be effectively utilized later.

In recent decades, land has been the principal crop of farmers living near cities; many farms have been sold to real estate developers for sums far exceeding what the land was worth for agricultural production. But the movement of farms farther and farther from markets in the cities has caused some concern. Wolf Von Eckardt, architecture and planning critic, has pointed out that "In the long run this matter cannot be left entirely to chance and individual initiative." Agriculture can be maintained in the vicinity of cities, Von Eckardt asserts, "only if we distribute the land more wisely than now." One answer to the problem is agricultural zoning to protect farm land and its owners from rising taxes. Programs of this type have been introduced in California and in a part of Lancaster County, Pennsylvania.[23]

Similar techniques can be used to preserve open space for recreational activities. The Outdoor Recreation Resources Review Commission has cited a number of devices, other than outright purchase, that can be employed to ensure future availability of land for outdoor recreation. The devices include purchase of land to be leased back for a particular use, thus providing control at a small cost. Another method is acquisition of an easement on property under which the owner agrees, for a cash payment or tax abatement, not to use his property in a manner that would destroy the possibilities for recreational development. Still

---

[22] Claiborne Pell, "The Case for High-Speed Trains in Inter-City Travel," *Perspective*, Third Quarter 1964, p. 4.

[23] Wolf Von Eckardt, *The Challenge of Megalopolis* (1964). p. 53.

other devices include exclusive agricultural zoning modified to allow hunting or similar recreational pursuits, and a requirement that property owners planning to sell give the local government advance notice of their intention and offer it first refusal rights.

So-called cluster development of suburban communities avoids dividing the land into plots of uniform size and shape. By grouping small house sites around cul-de-sacs and utilizing natural contours, a larger amount of land can be retained in its natural state as marsh, woods or streams, or can be reserved for parks and play areas. In communities so planned, many popular recreational activities, such as walking or picnicking, can be carried on close to home.

CONCEPT OF 'NEW TOWNS' OUTSIDE THE BIG CITIES

While cluster development may meet open-space and recreational requirements for relatively low-density regions, many developers and planners believe that "the answer to megalopolis" lies in establishment of new towns at a distance of 20 to 50 miles from the large cities. The new town concept has been given official support since 1946 in Great Britain, where 18 new communities are now in various stages of development.

The new town concept, which resembles the garden city concept in vogue before and after World War I,[24] is designed to allow high-density population development while providing urban services and employment for the inhabitants in an attractive open setting. Three new towns are in stages of advanced planning or initial construction near Washington, D. C. In contrast to the British pattern, all of these new towns are private developments. Already open to prospective home buyers and industry and government employers is Reston,[25] situated a score of miles northwest of Washington in the Virginia countryside. Reston, when completed in 1980, will house 75,000 inhabitants in seven villages. The community will feature an urban town center with a 16-story apartment tower, an artificial 35-acre lake for boating, swimming and fishing, new schools, a youth center, passageways and walkways separated from motor roadways, and recreational facilities such as a golf course and tennis courts.

---

[24] See "City Beautiful," *E.R.R.*, 1964 Vol. I, pp. 174-175.
[25] Named from the initials of developer Robert E. Simon.

Reston's success or failure may be a key to the future use of land in densely populated areas. Already a number of town houses, clustered around the lake, have been sold; prices range from $23,000 to $46,400. Six industrial enterprises have contracted to locate in the community's industrial park, and a federal government agency is considering locating there.

Other new towns slated for development in the Washington area are St. Charles City, a community planned for 8,000 acres about 25 miles to the southeast in Maryland, and Columbia, the largest of the three, about half way between Washington and Baltimore.[26] St. Charles City is to feature houses in a wider price range than at Reston—with some as low as $15,000 and others as high as $100,000. The city's backers have offered a 100-acre site free of cost to the General Services Administration for a new Government Printing Office that would employ 7,200 persons.

The developers of the new towns have managed to obtain private funds for the projects. But bankers and investors have to some extent been wary of the new developments. The reaction of the public is an unknown quantity despite the enthusiastic acclaim of planners and others. Federal assistance for the new communities was contemplated by President Johnson when he asked Congress in January 1964 to approve a program of grants and loans to state and local governments for planning of public facilities in anticipation of population growth and for advance land purchases. Johnson also proposed federal insurance of loans to private developers for construction of public facilities and the acquisition and improvement of land for planned subdivisions. None of these proposals won final approval by Congress. But H.H.F.A. Administrator Weaver hinted last Jan. 15 that the administration might renew the recommendations in the present Congress. Weaver told a meeting of the Highway Research Board that planned communities would meet the challenge of urban sprawl and contribute to orderly metropolitan development.

MEANS OF DEVELOPING HETEROGENEOUS COMMUNITIES

One aspect of the new towns that causes concern is the possibility that they may become upper middle or upper class enclaves that would exclude lower income and non-

---

[26] Columbia is planned to house a population of 110,000.

white groups. Bernard Weissbourd, president of a construction company, has asserted that the government should
take steps to assure development of new towns as heterogeneous communities from both a racial and an economic
standpoint. He proposed that Federal Housing Administration and Veterans Administration regulations prohibiting discrimination because of race be applied to mortgage
loans by savings and loan associations; that F.H.A. loan
guarantee programs for middle-income housing be made
available in new towns; and that each new town be required
to provide a minimum of public housing and housing for
the elderly as a condition of eligibility for federal loan guarantees. These federal tools, he concludes, "would be powerful inducements for the creation of heterogeneous new towns
in which individuals and industry displaced from the city,
together with some of the 80 million new people to be housed
between now and 1980, could be accommodated." [27]

PLAN FOR HIGH-SPEED TRAINS IN NORTHEAST CORRIDOR

Of special interest to the long-distance commuters of
Megalopolis, and of potential interest to the remainder of
the nation, is the growing support for rapid rail transportation in the corridor from Boston to Washington. Extensive inter-city travel in this region prompted President
Kennedy to initiate a study by the Commerce Department
of the dual problem of improving existing passenger transportation facilities and developing new and much faster rail
passenger service. Preliminary recommendations were submitted to President Johnson last Aug. 11. The President
then asked for further study of engineering and cost data
for development of a high-speed rail system as well as an
economic analysis of the benefits that might be gained
from it.

The technical study, undertaken by the Massachusetts
Institute of Technology, is due to be completed next June.
But a preliminary study, submitted by M.I.T last October,
concluded that the benefits would be substantial not only for
the Northeast Corridor but also for the country as a whole.
The President on Jan. 25 asked Congress to appropriate $20
million for further research and for testing and demonstration projects.

The godfather of the Northeast Corridor project, Sen.

---

[27] Bernard Weissbourd, *Segregation, Subsidies, and Megalopolis* (1964), p. 9.

Claiborne Pell (D R.I.), hopes that the study will lead to creation of an eight-state public authority to operate the proposed rail passenger service. Pell on Jan. 6 reintroduced his bill to authorize creation of a new agency to undertake rehabilitation of the existing railroad system in the area when it is possible to implement the findings of the research program.

The Pell plan for an interstate compact and a multi-state public authority is not the only solution, but the senator considers it "a reasonable and practical approach." [28] The authority would issue long-term, low-interest bonds, with a federal guarantee, to raise funds to finance necessary improvements in existing track and roadbeds and purchase of the new equipment necessary for high-speed rail travel. Sen. Pell believes that a system of trains moving at speeds of more than 100 miles an hour and operating at short headway—perhaps a departure from Washington and Boston every 15 minutes—could win automobile and air travelers back to the rails. The expectation is that travel time from Washington to New York could be cut from the present three and one-half or four hours to two hours, and the time from Washington to Boston from eight and one-half hours to four hours. A high-speed rail line between Tokyo and Osaka, Japan, with trains operating at speeds of up to 125 miles an hour, was put in service last October.

NEED TO COORDINATE DEVELOPMENT OF MEGALOPOLIS

Despite a proliferation of planning agencies in the United States, there is little over-all coordination—and little authority to bring about adherence to the plans that are made. Wolf Von Eckardt has noted that a part of the problem is political:

> Comprehensive regional planning to guide the development of Megalopolis and assure its livability is the great, over-riding challenge. We have planning for small units such as city and suburban neighborhoods and urban renewal projects. But these pieces do not yet make a clear, workable and attractive mosaic. Nor is comprehensive regional planning of much use if it remains a theoretical exercise confined to study groups, commissions, and boards with insufficient political and popular support to make it effective.[29]

Two Duke University professors, Robert H. Connery and

---

[28] Rep. Paul A. Fino (R N.Y.) has proposed creation of a federal authority to control and subsidize all forms of passenger transportation—rail, bus and air—between southern Maine and northern Virginia.

[29] Wolf Von Eckardt, *op. cit.*, p. 121.

Megalopolis: Promise and Problems

Richard H. Leach, fear there is danger that metropolitan planning agencies "will be divorced from a meaningful political base." They think that a representative body of local elected officials should be involved in the planning process.[30]

A requirement that all federally assisted projects be meshed with central development plans would be a step toward achieving the necessary coordination. Such a requirement has been advocated by the Advisory Commission on Intergovernmental Relations as well as by various planning bodies. The Metropolitan Conference Committee of the American Institute of Planners proposed in 1962 that to coordinate local plans with metropolitan plans, and metropolitan plans with state and national programs, "there should be a legal requirement that the [local planning] agency review the content, conformity, or compatibility of all proposals affecting the metropolitan area."

---

[30] Robert H. Connery and Richard H. Leach, "Southern Metropolis: Challenge to Government," *Journal of Politics*, February 1964, p. 79.

▼ ▼ ▼

VIOLENCE IN AMERICAN LIFE

by

Joan S. Gimlin

1 9 6 8
June 5

VIOLENCE IN AMERICAN LIFE

IF VIOLENCE, in the words of Negro militant H. Rap Brown, is "as American as cherry pie," [1] realization of that fact comes as a shock to a country which has prided itself on being "the land of the free and the home of the brave." The nation's tremendous resources and the vigor of its polyglot population usually made it possible in the past to allay group tensions without great difficulty. That has become almost impossible in a time of nationwide outbreaks of racial rioting, student rebellions across the country, and endless anti-war and anti-draft demonstrations and parades.

Violence in the United States has become the subject of constant and at times obsessive discussion, not because it is new in American life but because it is different. "It is greater, more real, more personal, suffused throughout the society, associated with not one but a dozen issues and causes. It is invoked by the most rational, public and respected of our institutions, as well as by the most obscure and piteous lunatic." [2]

Horrors of the war in Viet Nam expand, rioting spreads in the ghettos, the assassination of a President is followed by the assassination of the leading Negro spokesman for non-violence, and suburban housewives go shopping for guns. "The sheer effort to hold things together has become the central issue of politics in a nation that began the decade intent on building a society touched with moral grandeur." [3]

INTENSIFICATION OF TENSION BETWEEN THE RACES

The nation's white population has reacted to the latest racial threats by indulging in a wave of gun buying estimated to have brought the total of guns in American homes to around 50 million. The arson and looting that occurred in

---

[1] Remark by the chairman of the Student Nonviolent Coordinating Committee at Washington, D. C., rally, July 27, 1967. The rally followed Brown's release on bail in connection with extradition proceedings arising from charges that he had incited a riot in Cambridge, Md., two days earlier.

[2] Daniel P. Moynihan (head of M.I.T.-Harvard Joint Center for Urban Studies), "Has This Country Gone Mad?", *Saturday Evening Post*, May 4, 1968.

[3] *Ibid.*

cities all over the country after the murder of the Rev. Martin Luther King Jr. were of unprecedented extent. At the same time, the disturbances could be viewed as only the renewal of a series of race riots that began as early as 1741. Rumors then that slaves and poor whites were conspiring to burn down New York City touched off rioting in which 13 Negroes were burned alive; 101 Negroes and four whites were convicted of criminal arson, and 18 Negroes and four whites were hanged.

Resistance to the Civil War draft, which fell most heavily on the poor, and fear among Irish working people that freed Negro slaves would flood northern cities and deprive them of employment led to rioting in New York City in July 1863 that took the lives of more than 1,000 persons and injured an estimated 8,000.[4] White fear of Negro competition for jobs was a factor in race riots in numerous cities during and after World War I—in East St. Louis, Ill., in 1917 (47 killed); in Washington, D. C. (six killed), Chicago (36 killed), New York City, Omaha, and several southern cities in 1919; [5] and in Tulsa, Okla., in 1921. Race riots in Detroit in 1943, in the midst of World War II, took 29 lives.

The Negro's frustrations have been largely expressed through violence toward his own race. The Negro arrest rate for murder is 10 times the white rate, but most of the victims are Negro. Prior to World War I, most Negro leaders advocated accommodation with whites, largely because "Negroes had practically no resources or opportunities for protest and little support from any segment of the white population." Under the circumstances, vigorous protest activities would have been "both futile and dangerous, perhaps suicidal." [6]

Ironically, the country's major wars have been the occasion for Negro breakthroughs. The boom times and labor scarcity of two world wars and the Korean War gave Negroes an opportunity to find jobs in the promised land of the big cities. Southern Negroes migrated to northern cities in large numbers during and following the wars. By the late 1950s, however, the increasing automation of industry left fewer and fewer jobs for poorly educated, unskilled Negroes, and mechanization of agriculture was depriving more and

---

[4] See "Protest Movements in Time of War," *E.R.R.*, 1966 Vol. I, pp. 154-155.

[5] Samuel Eliot Morison, *The Oxford History of the American People* (1965), pp. 884-885.

[6] Leonard Broom and Norval Glenn, *Transformation of the Negro American* (1965), p. 8.

more Negroes in the South of opportunities to make a living on farms.

Although white liberals and middle-class Negroes led by such groups as the National Association for the Advancement of Colored People gradually achieved more legal equality for the Negro, the ghetto inhabitant and the farm laborer alike found little or no improvement in their lives. Or as Dr. Martin Luther King Jr. once remarked, "What good does it do to be able to eat at a lunch counter if you can't buy a hamburger?" Thus as most recent critics, including the National Advisory Commission on Civil Disorders, have noted, hope and acceptance in the ghetto faded as promises and new laws failed to work changes for the better.

The commission, which reported in March 1968, warned that many Negroes had come to feel that there was "no effective alternative to violence as a means of achieving redress of grievances." It added:

> We found that violence was generated by an increasingly disturbed social atmosphere, in which typically not one, but a series of incidents occurred over a period of weeks or months prior to the outbreak of disorders. . . . These earlier or prior incidents were linked in the minds of many Negroes to the pre-existing reservoir of underlying grievances. With each such incident, frustration and tensions grew until at some point a final incident, often similar to the incidents preceding it, occurred and was followed almost immediately by violence.

One student of urban violence has pointed out that violence in American cities is nothing new. "In the United States, our record of urban outbreaks should have taught us by now to expect inner-city mayhem among those whose lives are seared by misery and burnt-out hopes," wrote Dennis Clark. "It is the Irish who wrote the script for American urban violence, and the black terrorists have not added anything particularly new." In the decades from 1830 to 1870 the Irish "caused riots in almost every major city." [7]

PRESSURES OF WAR AND THE STUDENT REBELLION

Never before have Americans lived through a war in which so many have been so unsure of what "victory" will mean and whether it is worth having. The country has found it increasingly difficult to win either the physical war on the battlefield in Viet Nam or the psychological war on

---

[7] Dennis Clark, "Urban Violence: An American Institution," *America* (published by the Jesuits of the U. S. and Canada), June 1, 1968, p. 728.

the home front. Every war has had its dissenters and the equivalent of draft card burners, but the pressures of the Viet Nam war have become so great that President Johnson's decision not to seek another term can be viewed as one of the results.

For the hawks—those who support the war as necessary to the vital interests of the nation—the situation is frustrating because "the United States is facing in South Viet Nam . . . a primitive nation-in-arms, in a war which can be won only by incapacitating the total population." [8] In a war such as this "the guerrilla is indistinguishable from the rest of the population" and the superior U. S. military machine is stalled. Massive bombing is not effective in a country which has so few complex industrial and military sites, and the superior power is reduced to physically destroying the country in the effort to save it. For the doves—those who reject the war—the resort to napalm bombing, defoliation of crops, and maintenance of detention camps for large parts of the civilian population are repulsive elements of American war policy. Instead of being able to unite against the common enemy, Americans bitterly argue whether the enemy is really the Viet Cong or a misguided American foreign policy.

The war has been a substantial factor in sparking student campus protests; students have objected to current draft policies and to recruiting campaigns conducted by the armed forces on various campuses. But student protest has spread beyond these issues, notably at Columbia University where the basic authority of the university administration has been challenged. The president of the university, Dr. Grayson Kirk, announced May 25 that he would not deliver the commencement address on June 4 because students had threatened to disrupt the ceremonies. Although changes will be made in university policies, Kirk emphasized that students could not be granted substantial policy-making power. He emphasized that he would discipline, suspend or expel "any number" of students to restore order. A total of 998 students were arrested and more than 200 injured in the series of disorders on the Columbia campus that began April 23.

President Johnson addressed himself to campus violence in a speech on May 29 at Texas Christian University in

---

[8] Hans J. Morgenthau, "U. S. Misadventure in Vietnam," *Current History*, January 1968, p. 31.

Fort Worth. "Those who glorify violence as a form of political action are really the best friends the status quo ever had," the President declared. "They provoke a powerful conservative reaction among millions of people. They inspire, among many people, a blind allegiance to things as they are—even when those things should be changed."

RISE IN CRIME RATES; GUN CONTROL CONTROVERSY

The F.B.I. has reported that the combined incidence rate for violent crimes rose by 31 per cent between 1960 and 1966. The chief of the Los Angeles Police Department pointed out a few years ago that the United States had "the dubious distinction of being the most lawless of the world's nations, and the statistical experts foretell a continued increase." [9] According to one commentator, it is "our failure to control the indiscriminate sale and use of guns which in recent years has lain at the heart of the controversy and at the same time has made it politically insoluble."

A Louis Harris poll conducted in April 1968 indicated that 71 per cent of the American public favored passage of federal gun control laws. The survey analysts therefore concluded that a majority of the many Americans who have armed themselves would favor some other means of protection. The gun control provisions of the crime control bill passed by the Senate on May 23, 1968, represent the first significant step toward federal gun control legislation in 30 years. The provisions are limited to prohibition of interstate mail-order sales of handguns—pistols and revolvers—to individuals; banning of over-the-counter sales of handguns to non-residents of a state or to persons under 21; and curbing of imports and sales of surplus military weapons such as bazookas, mortars and antitank guns. There is no provision for regulation of sales of rifles or shotguns across state lines, and the House version of the crime control bill, passed by that body on Aug. 8, 1967, contained no gun control provisions at all.

A well-financed and highly vocal anti-gun control lobby led by the National Rifle Association has long opposed effective control legislation, particularly provisions for gun registration. According to an N.R.A. vice president, "Registration of firearms is a misguided step toward a police state

---

[9] Quoted by Richard Harris, "Annals of Legislation; If You Love Your Guns," *The New Yorker*, April 20, 1968, p. 56.

which never should be taken in a free country such as the United States of America." [10]

The image of what *Time* recently called "America the Violent" has been produced largely by the portrayal of violence in the movies and on the TV programs which are merchandised at home and in foreign countries. The legend of American violence has been so all-pervasive that more than one foreign visitor has expressed surprise at not being able to get a first-hand look at rampaging cowboys, Indians or gangsters. Americans have laughed at these misunderstandings, but any brief survey of the casual and constant use of violence in the mass media gives little grounds for assurance.

VIOLENCE IN TELEVISION SHOWS AND THE MOVIES

While adults argue the issues, the children are being conditioned. The National Association for Better Broadcasting in its 18th annual report on television programs for children, in March 1968, concluded that television for children was "a mass of indiscriminate entertainment dominated by some 40 animated program series" distinguished for "ugliness, noise and violence." Psychiatrist Fredric Wertham, long-time foe of violence in the mass media, has warned: "Our children have been conditioned to an acceptance of violence as no civilized nation has ever been before. . . . Children have an inborn capacity for sympathy. But that sympathy has to be cultivated. This is one of the most delicate points in the education process. And it is this point that the mass media trample on." [11]

A prediction made by Wertham some 30 years ago, that violence among children would increase, has become reality. The Leopold-Loeb murder case of a generation ago was sensational for the very reason that it was almost unheard of for an 18-year-old boy to commit sadistic murder; today, "murder by much younger youths has become commonplace" in this country, and murder committed by children under 14 is not a rarity. "It is not uncommon to see deliberate murder committed by children of 12 or 13 or even younger. Children of eight or nine are found torturing one another or committing serious acts of sadism." [12]

---

[10] Statement of Woodson D. Scott before Senate Subcommittee on Juvenile Delinquency, Committee on the Judiciary, July 19, 1967.

[11] Fredric Wertham, *A Sign for Cain—An Exploration of Human Violence* (1966), p. 210.

[12] *Ibid.*, p. 270.

The disturbed child may be most susceptible to the violence he sees. There is ample clinical evidence that all children exposed to acts of violence are over-excited by them and will tend to imitate what they see, rather than being drained of their aggressions. Eleanor Fischer, chief psychiatric social worker at the Army's Walter Reed Child Guidance Clinic, has noted that "Sick sadism in motion pictures can very definitely be damaging to a normal child's development."

Although violence has been present in the arts throughout history, many critics agree that a significant change is now taking place; as former *New York Times* movie critic Bosley Crowther has put it, "Moviemakers and movie-goers are agreeing that killing is fun—killing of a gross and bloody nature, often massive and excessive, done by characters whose murderous motivations are morbid, degenerate and cold." In New York City alone, the number of theaters which show sex-violence films exclusively has increased from 10 in 1966 to more than 25 today.

Sen. Margaret Chase Smith (R Maine) has been trying for more than a year, with little apparent success, to promote a system of film classification that would bar children from theaters showing clearly objectionable films. Film censorship laws have been disappearing since the Supreme Court, citing the First Amendment guarantee of free speech, ruled in 1952 that the New York Film Licensing Board could not ban an Italian film, *The Miracle,* on the ground that it was sacrilegious. Sen. Smith, while stressing that she does not favor general censorship, says she is "offended that boys and girls today are increasingly exposed to such sick violence for the sake of the quarters and dollars they contribute to America's $3 billion-a-year motion-picture industry." [13]

Americans who find movie carnage entertaining cannot take refuge in a non-violent past. Gangsters were being idealized long before Bonnie and Clyde became a successful movie and a national fad. Even that euphemistically labeled "children's book" *Huckleberry Finn* is a medley of violence that includes murder, feuds, drunken beatings, and mob action. In the words of Leslie Fiedler, Mark Twain is "a great poet of violence; and indeed, even his humor depends

[13] Margaret Chase Smith, "Sick Movies—A Menace to Children," *Reader's Digest,* December 1967.

upon a world in which there is neither a stable order nor civil peace." [14] The current danger lies in the fact that the boy hero is being replaced in the popular arts by the sadist who beats his lady-love with a bicycle chain.

Sources of Violence in American Life

AFTER TWO HUNDRED YEARS the American Revolution has been thoroughly legitimatized. "Yet it has always been difficult to conceal the fact that the nation was conceived in violence, that its birth was accompanied by mobs and confiscations, and that a burden remained on the people collectively to validate their rebellion against lawful authority." [15]

The Sons of Liberty was an essentially middle-class group of revolutionaries which provided radical leadership for lower class groups who formed the mob. Samuel Eliot Morison has written that at the time of the enactment of the Stamp Act in 1765 "These liberty boys . . . coerced distributors into resigning, burned the stamped paper, and incited people to attack unpopular local characters." On the day the Stamp Act went into effect "a howling New York mob" forced the colony's British governor to take refuge on a warship and then looted and destroyed the property of the resident British garrison. The scene was repeated, with variations, in other seaport towns—Charleston, Boston, Newport. Mob action, controlled by the Sons of Liberty, succeeded in nullifying the Stamp Act. "It was," concluded Morison, "an amazing exhibition of what a closely knit revolutionary organization could do, anticipating the Jacobins of the French Revolution and the Bolsheviks of the Russian." [16]

Even the celebrated Boston Massacre on March 5, 1770, appears to have been not the wanton slaughter of innocent citizens but the result of mob harassment of British troops, a few of whom were finally provoked into firing into the mob. Incidents such as these were exploited by the radicals to build up revolutionary sentiment. But occasionally the mob frightened American leaders themselves.

---

[14] Leslie Fiedler, *Love and Death in the American Novel* (Rev. ed., 1966), p. 275.
[15] David Brion Davis, "Violence in American Literature," *Annals of the American Academy of Political and Social Science*, March 1966, p. 30.
[16] Samuel Eliot Morison, *op. cit.*, pp. 186-187.

Violence in American Life

John Adams wrote in his *Autobiography* of a disturbing encounter with a habitual debtor who was looking forward to a new state in which there would be no courts of justice. Adams asked:

> Is this the object for which I have been contending? said I to myself, for I rode along without any answer to this wretch. Are these the sentiments of such people, and how many of them are there in the country? Half the nation for what I know. . . . If the power of the country should get into such hands, and there is **great** danger that it will, to what purpose have we sacrificed our time, health, and everything else? Surely we must guard against this spirit . . . or we shall repent of all our conduct.

Before the responsible leadership there was always the specter of the mob uncontrolled. In 1764 a band of 1,500 frontier hoodlums known as the Paxton Boys marched on Philadelphia, bent on killing Indians who had taken refuge there. The city panicked, "and it took Ben Franklin to talk the ruffians into going home, by promising more **frontier** protection and legislative bounties for Indians' scalps." [17] More than one leader wondered publicly if there were too many furies abroad to be controlled by any new republic.

VIOLENCE AND LAW ENFORCEMENT ON THE FRONTIER

Violence was a way of life on the frontier. One historian, describing the Scotch-Irish pioneers who settled the Virginia wilderness, said: "With one hand, as it were, they battled the irate landlords on whose lands they unceremoniously squatted, while with the other, they killed Indians and pushed back the forest." [18]

The first comers pressed ever forward through the wilderness, refugees from the restraints of established society. They furnished the stuff of the trapper and hunter legend, personified for later generations in James Fenimore Cooper's hero of the Leatherstocking tales. This figure was followed by the classic cowboy, the romantic stoic, immortalized in Owen Wister's *The Virginian*. For the settlers who followed the first wave, the frontier meant a hard scrabble with the land and efforts to establish solid and law-abiding communities. "The frontier was the low-rent district, the slums of colonial days. From the beginning the frontier also attracted outlaws, runaways, malcontents, freethinkers, and other

---

[17] *Ibid.*, p. 184.
[18] Carl Degler, *Out of Our Past* (1959), p. 52.

such undesirables." [19] Men were forced to rely on their own guns or the power of "lynch law" to control the criminal elements. The reality of the frontier was violent but not romantic; however, the heroic myth of the man with a gun has endured.

SLAVERY AND PATTERNS OF VIOLENCE IN THE SOUTH

America became heavily committed to slavery when that institution was coming to an end in most civilized countries. The intellectual elite who led in the founding of the nation were conscious of the gap between the professed ideals of the new democracy and the existence of slavery in their midst. By the early years of the 19th century, the practice had disappeared from the northern states, where it had proved unprofitable. Importation of slaves was prohibited by Congress in 1808, but by then slavery had come to be considered an integral part of the southern plantation system and it was to persist there for almost a half-century longer. In 1850, when the United States had a population of only 23 million, there were 3,200,000 slaves.

At the end of the Civil War, Congress created the Freedmen's Bureau to cope with problems of the newly freed Negroes, who were almost all illiterate, unskilled agricultural workers. The bureau promoted public education, including such Negro universities as Howard, Fisk, and Atlanta. Nearly 800,000 acres of confiscated or abandoned land and 5,000 pieces of similar town property were assigned to the Freedmen's Bureau and leased by it to former slaves, but most of the land was eventually restored to its former white owners. The bureau itself became deeply involved in politics and finally went out of existence in 1872.

After a decade of Reconstruction, new-found Negro freedoms were suppressed. Settlement of the disputed Hayes-Tilden presidential election contest of 1876 in favor of Hayes was followed by withdrawal of all federal troops from the South and termination of Reconstruction under northern auspices. Elimination of the few carpetbag governments then remaining completed restoration of state control to white southerners. They quickly found means to deprive Negroes of the right to vote. Progress toward full re-establishment of white supremacy had already been made during Reconstruction by secret strong-arm societies, notably the Ku Klux Klan.

---

[19] Alvin Josephy Jr., ed., *The American Heritage Book of Indians* (1961), p. 196.

A white Mississippian growing up in the 1950s has testified to the continuing patterns of violence inherited by southern society:

> Sports usually managed to soften the edge of violence that somehow hovered around us there, that crazy pent-up destructiveness that would sometimes erupt in fist-fights for no reason, or a frenzied and indiscriminate shoving, stomping and kicking. Two boys in the school, over a period of two years, killed their mothers, and a third, several years younger, later killed his grandmother in an old plantation house. . . . That curious Mississippi apposition—of courtliness and extraordinary kindliness on the one hand, and sudden violence on the other—was a phenomenon which never occurred to me.[20]

Mississippi today may be more typical of the old rural South than other southern states. However, a tendency toward unpredictable outbursts of temper or violence, whether a heritage from earlier times or a characteristic attributable to the climate, is still not uncommon among people in other parts of the region.

REMOVAL OF INDIAN TRIBES TO WESTERN TERRITORY

Indians tolerated the original white colonies founded along the Eastern seaboard. By the time they realized their mistake, white men were too firmly entrenched to be driven out. Killing Indians became, as Samuel Eliot Morison has noted, a part of the American way of life.

Displacement of the Indians had the inevitability of fate about it. President James Monroe wrote in 1817, "The hunter or savage state requires a greater extent of territory to sustain it, than is compatible with the progress and just claims of civilized life . . . and must yield to it." Methods of Indian treatment did not have the inevitability of fate, however; calculated brutality was the most frequent way of dealing with the Indian.

A removal policy became the law of the land in 1830 when President Andrew Jackson signed the Indian Removal Act. Under its terms all tribes east of the Mississippi River were to cede their lands in exchange for western territory. The Choctaw began the march followed by the Chickasaw. Although a treaty signed with the Creeks stipulated that no members of that tribe would be forced to move, "They were driven off their lands and forcibly set on the road west, their recalcitrant chiefs chained and handcuffed." [21]

---

[20] Willie Morris, *North Toward Home* (1967), pp. 125-127.
[21] Alvin Josephy Jr., *op. cit.*, p. 236.

Shortly after the Creeks arrived on their new lands, 3,500 out of a tribe of 15,000 died from disease and exposure. More than 4,000 out of 13,000 Cherokees also died on the "trail of tears." Treaties with the Indians continued to be made and broken. The Choctaw removal agreement stated that "no part of the land granted them shall ever be embraced in any territory or state." But in 1907 Choctaw land was among lands of various tribes that became part of the state of Oklahoma. In California, suppression of Indians was so effective during the Gold Rush that the native population was reduced by some 50,000 between 1849 and 1852.

TURBULENCE IN EARLY HISTORY OF AMERICAN LABOR

Violence in labor disputes has been more common in the United States than in other industrial countries. Despite attempts to deny the existence of classes within American society, labor disputes have often displayed elements of class warfare. During the early years of the nation, strikes were prevented, not only by lack of labor organization and the hostile attitude of the courts toward concerted labor activity, but also by the great shortage of skilled labor, by the payment of higher wages than working men had known in Europe, and by the fact that even discontented journeymen expected to become masters within a few years.

These barriers to violence began to disappear during the massive growth of the 19th century industrial machine. As John Mitchell, president of the United Mine Workers of America, phrased it in 1903: "The average wage earner has made up his mind that he must remain a wage earner. He has given up hope of a kingdom come, where he himself will be a capitalist."

Serious labor violence occurred in the prolonged depression that followed the panic of 1873. Even workers not laid off suffered wage cuts. Announcement of a 10 per cent cut by the Baltimore & Ohio Railroad in July 1877 set off a rail strike that spread across the nation. The militia was called out in several states, federal troops were sent in, mobs fought the soldiers, and fires were set. Community-wide riots "revealed the depth of the popular hatred of the rail barons." In Pittsburgh "almost the entire city turned out to loot and burn the railroad's property after the militia fired on the strikers." [22]

---

[22] Thomas R. Brooks, *Toil and Trouble, A History of American Labor* (1964), p. 53.

In the Pullman strike of 1894, which also led to a general rail strike, President Cleveland ordered federal troops to Chicago and to Oakland, Calif., to restrain mob violence and destruction of railroad property. Some 30 people were killed in the disorders. In all the major disputes "the strikers appeared to have been influenced by the feeling that the companies would not agree to any concession and . . . were determined to prevent the establishment of any representative organization." The employer intended to "remain absolute master in his own establishment." [23] Bloody strikes occurred in later years in all the major industries—mining, steel, clothing and lumber. Only since World War II has violence in labor disputes "appreciably diminished." [24]

Control of Aggression in Human Beings

MAN ALWAYS has compared himself and his behavior with the animals and animal behavior. Almost everyone has been exposed to animal fables and sayings such as "sly as a fox" and "gruff as a bear." But the revolutionary theories of biologist Charles Darwin first brought man's brotherhood with animals out of the realm of folklore and into the world of scientific exploration. A lifetime of animal study has recently led Konrad Lorenz, a biologist, zoologist and psychiatrist, to a revolutionary conclusion about the nature of animal life. Lorenz, who has been called the "father of modern ethology" [25] by Sir Julian Huxley, believes that animals and man possess a fundamental aggressive instinct, which is as basic as hunger and sex drives and which serves the purpose of conserving rather than of destroying the species.

Operation of the aggressive instinct in coral fish, for example, leads them to distribute themselves in suitable numbers over available territory. This "intra-specific aggression," directed primarily against members of the same species, operates for other vital purposes in animals such as bison, antelopes and horses, which form large herds and do not exhibit territorial jealousy. "Nevertheless the males of these species fight each other violently and dramatically, and

---

[23] Philip Taft, "Violence in American Labor Disputes," *Annals, op. cit.*, p. 130.
[24] *Ibid.*, p. 140.
[25] Ethology is a branch of biology concerned with the behavior of animals in their natural environment with special regard to the role of instinct.

there is no doubt that the selection resulting from this aggressive behavior leads to the evolution of particularly strong and courageous defenders of family and herd." [26]

Evolution and natural selection have at the same time given animals built-in inhibitions against destructive use of their instincts against their own. The larger and more predatory the animal, the stronger and more reliable are his inhibitions against killing others of the same species. Wolves and lions, for example, are among those possessing the most reliable inhibitions of this kind. Signals have evolved whereby when these animals fight their own to establish ranking order or sexual rights, they stop short of killing each other.

Paradoxically, only the more aggressive animals appear capable of forming personal bonds of affection, while the peaceable herd creatures remain all their lives in anonymous association. It is only man, standing at the forefront of animal development, who is in danger of suffering destruction from his aggressive instincts. His powers of verbal speech and conceptual thought have enabled him to invent sophisticated weapons and establish complicated social patterns, but his instincts for controlling his inventions have not kept pace with these products of his brain. "Evolution," Dr. Lorenz concludes, "is slower than cultural development by powers of ten—a million times slower, perhaps. Cultural development progresses quickly, but its very speed is dangerous. Thus the great question is: will man gain sufficient knowledge of himself before he destroys himself?" [27]

PSYCHOLOGICAL EXPLANATIONS FOR HUMAN VIOLENCE

Man, not the animal, systematically kills large numbers of his own species, his instincts being insufficient to restrain his capabilities. Perhaps the destructivity of man's aggressive drive evolved during the early Stone Age, after he had developed weapons, clothing and social organization, and after the danger of starving, freezing or being eaten by wild animals had been largely overcome. Then the previously "constructive" aggressive drive became the root of future tragedy as man turned increasingly on his own kind for reasons that were less than imperative.

Freud was the first student of human behavior to suggest that instinctive drives motivated man's actions. While many

---

[26] Konrad Lorenz, *On Aggression* (English translation, 1966), p. 39.

[27] Edward F. R. Sheehan, "Conversations with Konrad Lorenz," *Harper's,* May 1968, p. 74.

scientists accept his idea of constantly driving forces which must find release, Freud's belief in a death instinct has not been supported by research. Freud asserted that all living organisms had a tendency to seek the state of inorganic matter, to be relieved of all stimulation. If this were true, man's first tendency would be to commit suicide in order to end stimulation. According to Freud, all outward aggression in man was merely a redirection of this basic impulse to self-destruction. But research on animals and human behavior has shown that, contrary to Freud's theory, animals and man frequently seek an increase in excitement and stimulation. Or as the psychologist William McDougall phrased it, "The healthy animal is up and doing"—and apparently enjoying the activity.

McDougall and others favored a theory of aggression which stressed that hostile behavior had to be evoked by an appropriate stimulus. According to this view, it is only when normal self-preserving (goal-directed) activities are frustrated that the subject will respond with anger, and possibly with aggressive action. However, since man is a complex social animal, his feelings of anger may not necessarily erupt into hostile action. It depends on who or what the frustrator is, whether or not the victim expects to be punished or praised for aggressive action, and what his previously learned experience has been in frustrating situations.

Psychologists who favor instinctive theories of aggression are at odds with those who see violence as a reaction acquired in society. For the latter group, human violence is socially conditioned and socially preventable. Although the nature versus environment controversy is unsolved, anthropologists have succeeded in finding some groups of primitive men who enjoy life in relative peace. These include the Arapesh of New Guinea, Lepchas of Sikkim, and the pygmies of the Ituri rain forest in the Congo.

"All these societies," according to Geoffrey Gorer, "manifest enormous gusto for concrete physical pleasures—eating, drinking, sex, laughter—and . . . they all make very little distinction between the ideal characteristics of men and women. No child . . . grows up with the injunctions, 'All real men do . . .' or 'No proper woman does . . .' so that there is no confusion of sexual identity. . . . The model for the growing child is of concrete performance and frank enjoyment, not of metaphysical symbolic achievements or of ordeals to be surmounted. . . . A happy, hard-working and productive life is within the reach of all." [28]

While violence has been associated with primitive cultures, its most terrible excesses were reserved for the 20th century. Increasing acceptance of violence was mirrored in the literature of the 1930s, a process which critic Leslie Fiedler described as "the ennobling of violence as the 'midwife of history'."

> Under the name of "the revolution," violence becomes not something to be fled, not the failing of otherwise admirable men . . . but the climax of social action. The process which had begun just after 1789 with the Terror . . . received in an age of mechanized warfare and mass production its final form, . . . the twin horrors of Nazi and Soviet brutality; but a worse indignity had already been worked on the minds of the intellectuals, conditioned in advance to become apologists for one or the other system.[29]

Acceptance by the intelligent and the educated of violence as a tool of national policy led to conscious genocide in the modern police state. No one, said Fredric Wertham, can understand the "bureaucrats of genocide if he does not realize that as youths they learned, in most attractive literary form, such lessons as . . . the weak and misshapen have to perish. . . . The central message is that pity is weakness and cruelty is strength." [30]

America is familiar with the use of terror to control "troublesome" elements of the population. In most cases the commission of violent acts is entrusted to a special group which will do what the rest of the group does not wish to do directly. In Nazi Germany the S.S. (Schutzstaffel) or elite guard fulfilled that function. In the United States the urban police department has been a covert instrument for violence to the extent that it has resorted illicitly to third-degree methods to extort confessions. Policemen relied on to carry out such practices have been described as sadists. A sociologist who made a study of the modern police department reported:

> These few men seemed to be isolates, who aroused some revulsion and fear among their fellows. Yet, the ideological support of the use

---

[28] Geoffrey Gorer, "Man Has No Killer Instinct," *New York Times Magazine*, Nov. 27, 1966, p. 107.

[29] Fiedler, *op. cit.*, p. 484.

[30] Wertham, *op. cit.*, pp. 341-342. He refers here to the influential ideas of German philosopher Friedrich Nietzsche.

of violence among the police . . . made it difficult to organize support against them. They were, therefore, tolerated and, by implication, supported. Such sadistic men would boast of beatings which they had administered . . . and sometimes even about the many times they had killed.[31]

The moral climate of the world has made such atrocities as concentration camps and saturation bombings familiar in modern society. "Because it has been shown that the spirit of Hitler lives on in others as well, not merely in Germans; because susceptibility to totalitarian methods has become apparent throughout the world, . . . the atrocities of the past lose their deterrent effect among the wild horrors of the present . . ."[32]

NEED FOR SOCIAL CONTROL OF AGGRESSIVE TENDENCIES

In driving to achieve success and freedom, Americans have exhibited a curious mixture of idealism and greed. Democratic faith in freedom and equality has been genuine. Yet the grossest economic warfare and minority suppression have been bathed in sentimentality or rationalized as rugged individualism. Now, the old myths and sentimentalities are no longer able to mask the violence in society; the minority demands its rights and many of the young take advantage of the affluent world their parents created to reject parental values. For them the sexual and money problems that occupied their elders have been replaced by a confrontation with violence. "The issue of violence is to this generation what the issue of sex was to the Victorian world. . . . The fact of violent upheaval and the possibility of cataclysm . . . has been interwoven with the development of a whole generation."[33]

Social scientists, while differing over the origin of man's aggressiveness, agree that his behavior can be modified: "When angered, a seventeenth century nobleman might automatically reach for his sword, a nineteenth century cowboy for his gun, and a twentieth century Englishman for a pen so that he could write a letter to the *London Times*."[34]

William James proposed more than half a century ago a "moral equivalent of war" so that young men could exercise

[31] William A. Westley, "The Escalation of Violence Through Legitimation," *Annals of the American Academy of Political and Social Science*, March 1966, pp. 121-122.
[32] Eugen Kogon, *The Theory and Practice of Hell* (English ed., 1950), p. 290.
[33] Kenneth Keniston, "Youth, Change and Violence," *The American Scholar*, Spring 1968, pp. 242-243.
[34] Leonard Berkowitz, *Aggression; A Social Psychological Analysis* (1962), pp. 34-35.

their energies and develop hardiness and self-discipline without bloodshed. He proposed substituting a period of service for one's country—a sort of domestic Peace Corps.

In a speech entitled "Twentieth Century Violence and the Physician," social scientist Ashley Montagu warned that American parents are pressing the ideal of material success on their children to the exclusion of other ideals. He believes a lessening of these pressures would lead to a lowering of aggressive tensions among the young.

B. F. Skinner, a behavioral psychologist, has proposed an entirely new social organization. In *Walden Two,* group living is described as pleasant and profitable, children are raised as a group in a carefully controlled atmosphere of love and discipline, "superior" to the care of individual parents, and men and women participate equally in the work and leisure of the community. Man is manipulated by the state, but for his own benefit. The chief planner proclaims, "A laissez-faire philosophy which trusts to the inherent goodness and wisdom of the common man is incompatible with the observed fact that men are made good or bad and wise or foolish by the environment in which they grow." [35] Few would go as far as Skinner, but society is undoubtedly overdue for a debunking of the myth of the man with the gun as the embodiment of masculine virtue and glory.

---

[35] B. F. Skinner, *Walden Two* (1958), pp. 227-228.
[36] John W. Gardner, "Plain Talk About Hatred and Violence," *Reader's Digest,* June 1968, pp. 51-54.

LOCAL GOVERNMENT MODERNIZATION

by

Hoyt Gimlin

1 9 6 7
Oct. 11

LOCAL GOVERNMENT MODERNIZATION

LOCAL GOVERNMENT in the United States is being strained beyond its capacity to serve the great expanses of population building up in and around big urban centers. A frustration common to cities and suburbs is the inadequacy of existing governmental machinery to deal with the complexity and range of their problems. At the same time, the urban migration is depopulating the countryside to the point that local government is not easily supported in many rural areas.

The nation's top business leadership has recently expressed the belief that local government will gradually wither away unless it is reorganized in terms of 20th century needs. Its survival is considered essential on two grounds: first, the traditional one that government governs best when it is closest to the people; and second, that local government is necessary to the operation of federally financed programs across the nation.

The United States Chamber of Commerce is among business and public groups that within the past year have called for a political restructuring in city hall and county courthouse. The Chamber in May 1967 published a compilation of how-to-do-it ideas for community leaders. The Committee for Economic Development, whose membership also embraces the summit of American business, has warned against efforts merely to "tidy up a chaotic situation." The group's Research and Policy Committee recommended last year that the number of local governments be reduced by four-fifths. It considered that only the two newest states— Alaska and Hawaii—had "patterns of local government deliberately designed for modern conditions." [1] Many cities are hamstrung by unwieldy restrictions imposed by state constitutions and legislatures.

---

[1] C.E.D. Research and Policy Committee, *Modernizing Local Government* (1966), p. 26. The Chamber of Commerce compilation published in May 1967 bore the same title.

The Advisory Commission on Intergovernmental Relations, established by act of Congress in 1959, has said that a prime need of cities is the authority to extend their jurisdiction throughout metropolitan areas. "If one locality fails to control air or water pollution," the commission pointed out, "its neighbors suffer." [2] This fact was illustrated recently when the public works commissioner of Nassau County on Long Island charged that swarms of mosquitoes from New York City's adjoining borough of Queens had been invading Nassau communities. "Mosquitoes have no respect for boundary lines or home rule," the commissioner explained.

INCREASING FRAGMENTATION OF LOCAL GOVERNMENT

The Advisory Commission and others have voiced alarm at the growing fragmentation of local government and the resulting diffusion of control. The 1962 Census of Governments identified 91,187 local governmental units in the United States: 3,045 counties, 17,997 municipalities, 17,144 townships, 18,323 special districts, and 34,678 school districts. Special districts are the fastest growing, increasing by about one a day. They are usually set up for a single purpose—whether to provide fire protection, mosquito control, or garbage collection—and they frequently cross local boundaries. The special districts thus afford a means of working with the next-door suburb. But while necessary as expedients, they find disfavor with students of government because they impose overlapping layers of government, sometimes invisible to workaday citizens and often unresponsive to them.

Robert C. Wood, Under Secretary of Housing and Urban Development, has described the New York metropolitan area as harassed by "1,467 distinct political entities, each having its own power to raise and spend the public treasure, and each operating in a jurisdiction determined more by chance than design." [3] "The state of fragmentation," Wood added, "can be defended as carrying on the cherished democratic tradition of home rule. It can be deplored as hopelessly unsuited to the realities of modern metropolitan life."

Some urban specialists tend to think that only further fragmentation, toward a degree of self-government for

---

[2] Advisory Commission on Intergovernmental Relations, *Metropolitan America: Challenge to Federalism* (1966), p. 6.
[3] Robert C. Wood, *1400 Governments* (1961), p. 1.

neighborhoods, offers promise of surmounting the destructive forces that beset cities. Milton Kotler of the Institute for Policy Studies, in Washington, has made that point: "There is often little confidence in the city government. The neighborhood is the last unit of public confidence, and therefore, one must apply to that unit of public confidence the instrumentalities of legal self-governing and resources to act." [4]

The Committee for Economic Development, in contrast, clearly takes the view that local government is already too diffuse. It points out that fewer than one-half of all units of local government contain as many as 1,000 people; less than 10 per cent have more than 10,000, and less than 1 per cent have over 100,000. That means that few governmental units have the population base (50,000) that most experts regard as the minimum necessary to support efficient services.

"The basic local government structure in the United States," the National League of Cities has said, "was designed primarily for a rural, agricultural society whose inhabitants had a basic distrust of all governments." [5] The rural structure of government remains even though America has become an urban society.

GROWTH PATTERNS IN URBAN AND SUBURBAN AREAS

Today more than 70 per cent of the nearly 200 million Americans live in urban areas, up from 64 per cent in 1950. Of these urban dwellers nine of every ten are found in what the U. S. Census Bureau defines as the nation's 224 metropolitan areas.[6] The National Planning Association predicts that by 1975 some 164 million people, or 73 per cent of the expected population by that time, will live in metropolitan areas—with 60 per cent of the total concentrated in the 25 largest areas.[7]

The population has drained from the countryside into metropolitan areas but has not clustered in the central cities. Instead, the growth is spread around the suburbs, which are estimated to be growing five times as fast as the cities they encircle. This pattern of growth imposes major new service

---

[4] Milton Kotler, "Making Local Government Truly Local," *Trans-action*, October 1967, p. 50.

[5] National League of Cities, Department of Urban Studies, *Reorganizing Local Government for the Future* (June 1967), p. 9.

[6] A metropolitan area, formally a "standard metropolitan statistical area," generally is an area containing a central city of at least 50,000 people and its urbanized surroundings.

[7] *Looking Ahead* (publication of National Planning Association), June 1967, p. 1.

demands on local governments in outlying areas. The growing extent of these demands could be glimpsed in a special message on cities which President Johnson transmitted to Congress on March 2, 1965.

> Our new city dwellers [the President said] will need homes and schools and public services. By 1975, we will need over two million new homes a year. We will need schools for ten million additional children, welfare and health facilities for five million more people over the age of 60, transportation facilities for the daily movement of 200 million people, and more than 80 million automobiles.

> In the remainder of this century—in less than 40 years—urban population will double, city land will double, and we will have to build in our cities as much as all that we have built since the first colonist arrived on these shores.

While city and suburb alike face the demands President Johnson enumerated, and other demands, there has been little inclination to work together to meet them. This condition can be attributed in large part to the structure of government. "At no point is the structure of the American federal system of government so marked, varied and difficult as in the large metropolitan areas, where the activities of all three levels of government function in close proximity." [8]

SOURCES OF CONFLICT BETWEEN CITY AND SUBURBS

Political, social and economic differences between city and suburb abound. The city is likely to be governed by a single, tightly organized "strong-mayor" system, and the suburb by many relatively small units including numerous special districts. While the suburbs have grown rapidly, many large cities have lost population and experienced a marked change in racial composition. The white population increased in only eight of the nation's 20 largest cities in the 1950s, but the Negro population increased in every one of the 20 cities.[9] In a paper written for the Center for the Study of Democratic Institutions, Victor Palmieri, president of the Janss Corporation, has stated: "This, then, is the city of the future—the very near future: a black island spreading like a giant ink blot over the heart of a metropolis which is bankrupt financially and paralyzed politically."

Population changes suggest to many observers that metropolitan areas are becoming increasingly shaped along

---

[8] Advisory Commission on Intergovernmental Relations, *Government Structure, Organization, and Planning in Metropolitan Areas* (1961), p. 1.

[9] U. S. Bureau of the Census, "General Population Characteristics," *1960 Census of Population PC(1)B.*

racial and economic lines, intensifying the conflict between city and suburb. "Class and racial cleavages in metropolitan areas . . . foreshadow the next axis of antagonism in American politics: major alignments of the future will not be North vs. South or rural vs. urban, but city vs. suburban." [10]

Frances Fox Piven and Richard A. Cloward, faculty members at the Columbia University School of Social Work, see a pattern in federal aid that is "beginning to force localities to subordinate themselves to new area-wide planning bureaucracies." They conclude that the political power traditionally held by the inner city is in this way being diluted, and that the Negro will be deprived of real control even when his increasing numbers build up electoral majorities in the cities.

Piven and Cloward noted that the Department of Housing and Urban Development recently indicated it not only would require localities to cooperate in drawing up plans for "orderly metropolitan growth" but also would be prepared to withhold funds to enforce conformity with such plans. Moreover, they said, "Some of the larger federal programs are partly or wholly suburban-oriented: highways, airports, sewage and water facilities, mortgage insurance, and tax write-offs for homeowners."

The conflict between the city and the suburbs is already highly articulated in state legislatures. The two kinds of communities compete there for shared tax revenues; for financial aid for schools, welfare programs, and highways; for legislation which may benefit one metropolitan segment more than another. At the local level, cities and suburbs argue over who is subsidizing whom in matters of transportation services, zoning policy, health and welfare services, water pollution, and so on. "It often seems that the only common meeting ground lies in their reluctant partnership as the two halves of a statistical identity—the metropolitan area," the Advisory Commission on Intergovernmental Relations concluded. Thus loyalties remain local, giving rise to Prof. Roscoe A. Martin's observation: "Al Smith was from the sidewalks of New York, not the sidewalks of the New York-Northeastern New Jersey Standard Consolidated Area." [11]

---

[10] Frances Fox Piven and Richard A. Cloward, "Black Control of Cities," *New Republic*, Sept. 30, 1967, p. 21.

[11] Roscoe C. Martin, *Metropolis in Transition* (1963), p. 141.

"No city government collects anywhere nearly enough money of its own to take on the whole job of coping with all the problems that confront it." [12] That was the finding of a conference of city experts sponsored in New York last year by the National League of Cities, the American Institute of Architects, the Lincoln Foundation, and the Luce magazines. The conferees concluded that states were unwilling to grant cities the authority to tax heavily enough, that the cities were afraid to tax adequately even if they had the authority, because industry might move out, and that the almost exclusive reliance of cities on the property tax was self-defeating.

"Finally," the conferees reported, "nobody can tell just who is responsible for what. Schools, for example, are paid for partly by the local school district, partly by the state, a little by Washington, with the state setting the standards, the local authorities picking the teachers, and the federal government decreeing the racial balance."

RISING GOVERNMENT COSTS; NEED FOR NEW REVENUE

The financial plight of big cities is unquestionably abetted by the exodus of well-to-do whites and their money to the suburbs. In their place come the poor, bringing with them costly social problems. But a number of experts tend to believe that tax policies self-imposed by the cities are equally at fault. A group of tax specialists meeting at Claremont (Calif.) Men's College in 1964 had the following to say:

> None of us would dream of suggesting that local tax reform will cure all the ills of our cities. But most of us see a clear, close and causal connection between what is wrong with our cities today and what is wrong with the tax system. . . .
>
> If slums are spreading into what should be our fine close-in residential areas, how largely is this because old housing is so lightly taxed that it is more profitable to let it sink into slums? If our cities are disintegrating at their perimeters instead of expanding in an orderly way, how much of this sprawl is because under-used land on the outskirts is so lightly taxed that its owners feel no pressure to let it be put to better use when it is needed? If mass transportation is half empty and downtown is choked with parked private cars, to what extent is that due to the fact that our cities subsidize those who ride in cars by letting them on the downtown streets for a small fraction of the cost? [13]

The real property tax (as distinguished from the personal property tax) accounts for $7 of every $8 of revenue raised

---

[12] "What Kind of City Do We Want?" *Nation's Cities*, April 1967, p. 2.
[13] Cited in "The Great Urban Tax Tangle," *Fortune*, March 1965, p. 106.

locally across America. Mayors have argued, in an unending search for new sources of revenue, that their cities must supplement the property tax with a broad-based sales or income tax, or both. City sales taxes have become widespread, and the income tax, though largely pre-empted by the federal and state governments, is imposed by at least 40 large and middle-sized cities.[14]

Mabel Walker, executive director of the Tax Institute of America, in charting the rise of the local income tax has spoken of its "inevitability." [15] The "inevitability" of a new tax can be ascribed to the mounting cost of local government. The Committee for Economic Development reports that local expenditures, though varying widely from place to place, amount on the average to the equivalent of 10 per cent of personal income, 4 per cent more than 25 years ago. Public payrolls are growing fastest not at the federal but at local and state levels. State and local government employees numbered 8.6 million in October 1966, an increase of 7.7 per cent in 12 months, reflecting the growing demand for local services.[16]

Local Government in a Federal System

AMERICAN LOCAL GOVERNMENT is basically English in origin, although different patterns developed throughout the country because of varied geographic, economic and social conditions. New England settlements were relatively compact, and church congregations provided the focal point of society. Hence the village or unincorporated town became the dominant feature of local government. In the South the county accommodated a plantation society, and it remains, as in the sparsely settled West, the most important unit of government beyond the limits of the major cities of those regions.

The Middle Atlantic states and the Middle West have features of both the New England and southern systems. In New York, New Jersey, Pennsylvania, Michigan and Wis-

---

[14] See "Local Income Taxes and Revenue Needs," *E.R.R.*, 1966 Vol. I, p. 333.
[15] Mabel Walker, "The Inevitability of City Income Taxes," *Virginia Municipal Review*, March 1967, p. 41.
[16] See *Congressional Quarterly Weekly Report*, June 30, 1967, p. 1125.

consin the township continues to exercise governing functions. In the Middle West, independent school districts are a
prominent feature of local government, whereas in New
England they are more likely to be an integral function of
town government. Townships exist in the South, though
rarely with significant functions, but they are not found in
the Rocky Mountain states or in most of the Far West.

Municipalities also display a regional variation. The term
itself applies to all incorporated areas, whether they call
themselves cities, boroughs, towns or villages. However, a
borough in New York State is a sub-unit of a municipal
government; New York City is composed of the boroughs
of Manhattan, Brooklyn, Queens, Richmond (Staten Island)
and the Bronx. The degree of authority granted to the cities
is unevenly spread from state to state, and even from city to
city within a state. On the one hand, "The various local
governments are created by the individual states and remain
literally the creatures of the states." [17] But running counter
to the legal doctrine that local units of government are the
creatures of the state is the concept of home rule—local
control of local affairs. Today, some form of home rule is
granted by more than two-thirds of the states, but its extent
is strictly defined.[18]

EXTENT OF STATE RESTRICTIONS ON LOCAL AUTHORITY

The reluctance of state governments to yield control to
their offspring is a sore point with mayors, who want both
more taxing power and authority to deal with metropolitan-
wide problems. State constitutions are frequently criticized
as unduly restrictive, and state legislatures as unresponsive.
Aside from the new states of Alaska and Hawaii, only Connecticut, Georgia, Michigan, Missouri and New Jersey have
adopted new constitutions since 1945. However, New York
and Rhode Island voters will decide on Nov. 7 whether to
adopt or reject newly drafted state constitutions. Maryland
is currently holding a state constitutional convention, and
Pennsylvania opens a convention for limited revision of its
constitution on Dec. 1. Hawaii follows in 1968.

Constitutional revision, while welcomed by students of

---

[17] National League of Cities, *op. cit.*, p. 7.

[18] States having provisions of some kind for home rule include Alabama, Alaska,
Arizona, California, Colorado, Connecticut, Florida, Georgia, Kansas, Kentucky, Louis-
iana, Maryland, Michigan, Minnesota, Missouri, Nebraska, Nevada, New Jersey, New
Mexico, New York, North Carolina, Ohio, Oklahoma, Oregon, Pennsylvania, Rhode
Island, South Dakota, Tennessee, Texas, Utah, Virginia, Washington, West Virginia,
Wisconsin.

government, does not necessarily fulfill the cities' hopes. Mayor John V. Lindsay of New York City accused the constitutional drafters in his state of keeping cities in fiscal straits by refusing to enlarge home rule and taxing powers. He said the proposed changes in the state constitution offered his city no help in those areas.

State governments are relatively generous in allowing cities to go beyond their boundaries to obtain water or dispose of wastes. Many cities also exercise police powers beyond their borders in such health matters as milk or meat inspection. But rarely are they permitted to engage in outside planning or zoning—matters vital to orderly metropolitan growth. Even where this kind of authority exists, it is limited to unincorporated territory adjacent to the city— territory which scarcely exists any longer around urban centers.

In the matter of changing local boundaries, state laws usually require approval at the state level—by legislature or commission—and by the local electorate. On the other hand, local governments are usually free to enter voluntary and cooperative agreements that entail the exercise of some extraterritorial powers. This fact is attested by the relative ease with which special districts are formed. Their number rose by 50 per cent between 1952 and 1962.

If a special district crosses state lines, however, approval must be obtained from Congress and from the legislature of each state involved. Difficult as that process is likely to be, modern conditions have made resort to interstate compacts increasingly necessary. An example is the Port of New York Authority, established by New York and New Jersey in 1922 to promote commerce and manage transportation facilities on both sides of the Hudson River. Here, a multi-purpose function is undertaken, rare among special districts. An interstate compact, more often, is set up for a single purpose, perhaps the control of water in a river basin. The seven-state Colorado River Compact Commission, for example, allocates the river's water among the states under a set of complex formulas. Congress has removed the requirement of prior approval in one field of interstate agreements, that of building and maintaining airports serving more than one state, and it has been urged to do likewise in other fields.

Sometimes a state will assume functions that have grown beyond the reach of city or even metropolitan control. The State of California, for example, has taken over water development, tapping its northern rivers to quench the thirst of growing Southern California. Political scientists have mixed views about transferring metropolitan problems to state governments. The merit of doing so, they contend, is that the geographic base of planning and control is broadened. The drawback is that metropolitan matters are exposed to the disinterest, if not the outright opposition, of outsiders. The Eighth Annual Report of the Advisory Commission on Intergovernmental Relations (1967) concluded that only a handful of states had moved to meet the problems of their urban areas. It found that state governments were on the verge of losing control over the mounting problems of central city deterioration and the rapid growth of metropolitan areas.

LOCAL GOVERNMENT AND LEGISLATIVE REDISTRICTING

"Particularly since the depression of the 1930s, local governments have learned to take their problems to Washington rather than to the state capitols when they need outside help. . . . The unequal apportionment of state legislatures was important in weakening the political leverage of urban areas to the statehouse, while the strength of the metropolitan voters in national elections encouraged a more sympathetic hearing in Congress or the Executive Branch."[19]

A series of Supreme Court decisions beginning in 1962 with Baker *v.* Carr has led to widespread state legislative reapportionment on a basis of population.[20] But the impact upon the cities is still unclear. One observer has written: "Few central cities have felt the benefits of the *Baker-Carr* decision despite the reapportionment of 45 states. Instead of facing an implacably hostile alliance of rural legislators and their over-represented cows, cities now face a slightly less truculent coalition of rural legislators and those from suburbia, whose views on mass transit or education vary considerably from those of city dwellers." [21]

The Supreme Court has left in doubt whether its "one man, one vote" principle is applicable to legislative bodies

---

[19] Advisory Commission on Intergovernmental Relations, *Metropolitan America: Challenge to Federalism* (1966), pp. 117-118.

[20] Baker *v.* Carr, 369 U.S. 186 (1962). The Court held that federal courts had jurisdiction in cases of state legislative apportionment. Two years later, in Reynolds *v.* Sims (377 U.S. 533), came the doctrine of "one man, one vote."

[21] Martin Nolan, "Walter Heller's Federalist Papers," *The Reporter*, June 1, 1967, p. 16.

below the state level. On May 22 it upheld the unequal districting of a school board in Kent County, Mich., and a city council in Virginia Beach, Va. The Court also stopped short of ruling whether "one man, one vote" must be applied in the election of county boards of supervisors. It refused on procedural grounds to rule on this question in appeals from Suffolk County, N. Y., and Houston County, Ala.

At issue in Suffolk was a "weighted" voting plan under which five county supervisors representing populous towns cast 120 votes, while the other five supervisors cast only 14 votes. Previously, the latter five had had one-half of the board's 10 votes although they represented only 10 per cent of the county's 990,000 residents. After the Supreme Court sent the case back to the lower court, U. S. District Judge Walter Bruchhausen ordered a return to the old system of one vote per supervisor regardless of population. Bruchhausen said that "so far" the Supreme Court has not extended its "one man, one vote" rule to local government.

Increased Federal Involvement in Local Affairs

The federal system has sometimes been likened to a three-layer cake, an imagery that conveys the idea of national, state and local governments functioning apart and independently. But now the popular analogy is that of a marble cake, with a haphazard intermingling of all three levels of government. Sen. Edmund S. Muskie (D Maine), chairman of the Senate Government Operations Committee's Subcommittee on Intergovernmental Relations, has gone further and suggested that a large brick of ice cream containing a great number of flavors—one for each major existing federal aid program—would be more apt.

Historians differ as to whether the levels of government were intended to remain apart, but in this century the question has been made academic by Washington's increased involvement in local matters.[22] "The New Deal was crucial in shaping modern cooperative federalism," Harry N. Scheiber has written. "In the first place, it brought dramatic centralization of power, as the federal government responded to a depression crisis with sweeping labor, agricultural, public works and welfare programs."[23] Scheiber

---

[22] The late Prof. Morton Grodzins and Prof. Daniel J. Elazar, challenging a long-prevailing view, contended that cooperation among the levels of governments characterized the American political system from the beginning and that the "layer-cake" theory was always without validity.

[23] Harry N. Scheiber, *The Condition of American Federalism: An Historian's View* (study prepared for Senate Subcommittee on Intergovernmental Relations, Oct. 15, 1966), p. 8.

observed that the emergency relief agencies of the New Deal promoted a tendency, now in full flower, to bypass state capitols in distributing federal aid to local communities.

The bypassing has given rise to two sharply opposed views. "We have 50 years of history to prove the cities don't get a fair shake at the state capitols," John Gunther, executive director of the National Conference of Mayors, said in an interview in July 1966. "The picture of elected officeholders pleading their case and cause in a distant bureaucracy is not one which squares with our theories of representative government," said the Republican Coordinating Committee, a group headed by Rep. Robert Taft Jr. of Ohio, in a statement the same month. Scheiber has asserted that the bypassing will intensify as grants-in-aid increase, especially in school and poverty programs. In 1961, estimated federal obligations for direct expenditures and grants-in-aid affecting urban areas stood at $7.5 billion. In 1967 the urban budget was an estimated $16.4 billion and for 1968 the estimate is still higher at $19.4 billion. Monies for urban programs are rising twice as fast as the Gross National Product, and about 2½ times as fast as total federal spending.[24]

President Johnson, in Great Society proposals and in political speeches, has used the term "creative federalism," which he has defined as "the cooperation of the state and the city, and of business and labor, and of private institutions and of private enterprise." [25] While the dimensions of "creative federalism" remain uncertain, another concept of federal-state partnership has gained attention in Congress and elsewhere. This concept, brainchild of Walter W. Heller, former chairman of the President's Council of Economic Advisers, entails turning back a share of federal tax revenue to the states with few or no strings attached.[26] Mayors of big cities have opposed the Heller plan on the ground that state capitols have shortchanged cities for years and cannot now be entrusted to do better. The mayors who have testified before Congress on the Heller plan clearly prefer a continued bypassing of the state capitols unless their voices there become very much stronger.

---

[24] Estimates presented to a conference on The Next Fifty Years, held by the American Institute of Planners in Washington, Oct. 1, 1967, by Robert C. Wood, Under Secretary of the Department of Housing and Urban Development.

[25] Speech before members of New York Liberal party, Oct. 15, 1964.

[26] See "Federal-State Revenue Sharing," *E.R.R.*, 1964 Vol. II, pp. 943-946.

Action to Strengthen Local Government

ANNEXATION has been traditionally the most common method of adjusting the boundaries of local governments. Most of the nation's great cities achieved their present geographical limits through this process, but in recent decades the growing urbanization on their borders has made annexation more complicated. However, as recently as 1960, Kansas City, Mo., annexed 187 square miles, more than doubling its territory. Oklahoma City added 193 square miles to its 88 square miles in 1959, and the following year it added 149 square miles more. Major annexations of this type depend on two conditions, both rare: liberal state annexation laws and sizable surrounding territory that is still unincorporated.

California, Minnesota, Nevada and New Mexico have created commissions with power to approve or disapprove proposals for municipal annexation and incorporation. In California, where this type of commission is strongest, it is viewed as easing the way to formation of governmental units that will meet the needs of urban areas.

Consolidation, the merger of two existing units of government into one political structure, has been used in the United States only infrequently as a means of reorganization. It is forbidden by more than one-half of the states. Nevertheless, in the last century, city-county consolidation was achieved in Philadelphia (1854), Boston (1882), and New York (1898). Starting in the late 1950s a series of attempted city-county consolidations were defeated. These included: Albuquerque, N. M. (1959); Knoxville, Tenn. (1959); Macon, Ga. (1960); Durham, N. C. (1961); and Richmond, Va. (1961). Voters in Nashville and Davidson County, Tenn., rejected consolidation in 1958 but approved it four years later.

"As a way of adjusting boundaries to the geographical area of metropolitan problems, city-county consolidation has the greatest potential in medium and small metropolitan areas that are contained in one county and are unlikely to extend beyond the county's boundaries for some time to come," according to the Advisory Commission on Intergovernmental Relations. "A major weakness of the city-county

77

consolidation is that it has limited usefulness in metropolitan areas that are not confined in a single county." [27]

The consolidation device has been much more frequently applied to independent school districts, reducing the number of such districts by 75 per cent since 1942. Reduction to the present level of 25,000 has been attributed chiefly to state action, either mandated or pressured through school aid formulas. "Still, the number is too high," the Committee for Economic Development maintains. "Over 3,000 independent school districts do not maintain schools, having no children of school age or sending their few to other districts on a tuition basis. . . . About half of all independent school districts have less than 50 pupils, but these units account for only 1 per cent of public school enrollments."

EMERGENCE OF STRONG URBAN COUNTY GOVERNMENTS

The county, long a stepchild among urban governments, is now sometimes being championed as the city's needed big brother. The idea of strengthening the county to care for both city and suburban problems has been advanced by the Committee for Economic Development, the Republican Coordinating Committee, and the National Association of Counties.

Traditionally, the county has been more attuned to the rural-dominated statehouse than to its neighboring city, but evidence of change was reflected in the 1960 census showing of 263 counties each with 100,000 people or more. Strong county government is found in suburban New York, in Los Angeles, and in Dade County, Fla.[28]

Westchester, Nassau and Suffolk counties in New York have streamlined their boards of supervisors, established the post of county executive, and placed increased responsibility on county government. But cities within these counties continue their municipal existence virtually unchanged by the arrangement.

Los Angeles County carries out the urban county role on an even grander scale. Encompassing 4,000 square miles and 6.5 million people, it is the nation's most populous county. The City of Los Angeles accounts for about one-tenth of the total area; the remainder is filled by 75 satellite

---

[27] Advisory Commission on Intergovernmental Relations, *Metropolitan America: Challenge to Federalism* (1966), p. 104.
[28] See "Megalopolis: Promise and Problems," *E.R.R.*, 1965 Vol. I, pp. 110-111.

cities ranging from Long Beach (population 369,000) to the City of Industry (746).

The Los Angeles city government's framework is "too anachronistic for a central city, much less for coping with the problems of an incipient megalopolis," according to Richard Austin Smith. "Created at a time when reform groups across the nation were intent on stamping out boss rule, the Los Angeles charter is dedicated to the idea that the weaker the government the less harm it will do. Thus power is split between the mayor and a city council in such a way that neither can assume effective leadership." [29] Smith added:

> In contrast to the city's constricted governmental mechanism is the exemplary framework of Los Angeles County. Many people in Southern California have come to look on the county as a model of metropolitan government of the future. Its five supervisors represent more people—nearly 1,300,000 apiece—than their counterparts anywhere else in the U. S., and are almost too free of the checks and balances written into our system of government. They are executive and legislature all rolled into one and even function as a quasi-judiciary in the matter of zoning. Last year they spent nearly a billion dollars on such county-wide services as welfare, hospitals, jails, and the world's largest sheriff's office.

Under California's Lakewood plan, named for one of the municipalities in Los Angeles County, the county contracts to perform as many as 45 "local" services for individual cities. This practice has enabled a number of communities to incorporate which otherwise could have ill afforded to do so. The *Los Angeles Times* reported on June 25, 1967, that all except two of the 31 incorporated areas formed within Los Angeles County since 1954 had availed themselves of county services. Smith noted, however, that the "functional consolidation" of an urban county as practiced in Los Angeles was "a whole world removed from political consolidation."

TORONTO'S PIONEERING IN METROPOLITAN GOVERNMENT

True political consolidation is found in a federated system of city government carried on in at least two major Canadian cities, in Toronto since 1954 and in Winnipeg since 1960. Metropolitan Toronto, as that government is officially designated, is formed by the city and 12 suburbs united to assume areawide functions; purely local functions are left to each locality. Metropolitan Toronto is responsible for

---

[29] Richard Austin Smith, "Los Angeles, Prototype of a Supercity," *Fortune*, April 1965, p. 207.

police protection, water supply, sewage disposal, housing, tax assessment, arterial highways, metropolitan parks, some welfare services, and area planning.

The governing body consists of 12 Toronto officials and the council chairman of each of the 12 suburbs. They select a 25th member, who becomes the over-all chairman. Each suburban unit of the metropolitan government performs such local functions as water distribution, sewage collection, most health services, direct public relief, building inspection and local planning. School control remains primarily under the local government, but a metropolitan school board provides basic financing, planning and construction review.

The Toronto approach has been the subject of considerable study by American city officials and political scientists interested in the applicability of its features on this side of the border.[30] However, there is little evidence that urban America is favorably disposed to handing over actual political control to a metropolitan supergovernment.

"Every so often . . . metropolitan government is put up to the voters," urban critic Jane Jacobs asserts. "The voters inexorably and invariably turn it down. The voters are right in spite of the fact that there is great need for common and coordinated action. . . . The voters sensibly decline to federate into a system where bigness means local helplessness, ruthless, oversimplified planning, and administrative chaos —for that is just what municipal bigness means today." [31]

In addition, there is a natural reluctance to change. Property owners often assume that a change in the status quo will lead to higher taxes; officeholders fear loss of their jobs; residential communities fear zoning changes, and so on. Moreover, the average resident may be unaware of any real need for change.

> Experienced observers of the metropolitan scene may be acutely aware of the defects and potential dangers that lie in the present system, but the average citizen has little such consciousness. He may be dissatisfied with the performance of certain functions, he may desire better or additional services, he may wonder at times where all this explosive growth is leading and what it means in terms of his daily living, but he is not deeply troubled. He feels no impelling need, no urgency, for any restructuring of the governmental pattern of the area.[32]

---

[30] See "Metropolitan Government," *E.R.R.*, 1956 Vol. II, pp. 585-588.
[31] Jane Jacobs, *The Death and Life of Great American Cities* (1961), p. 427.
[32] John C. Bollens, *Exploring the Metropolitan Community* (1961), p. 70.

Local Government Modernization

Mayor Richard J. Daley of Chicago has demonstrated that a degree of metropolitan control may be achieved without an over-all governmental structure, William Bowen has observed. "Being a politician rather than a man in politics can be a great advantage to a mayor in getting things done," Bowen said. "A mayor's authority stops at the city line, but his city's problems sprawl on beyond; Daley has found it easier to deal with that difficulty than most mayors because, in addition to being mayor, he is chairman of the Cook County Democratic Committee, a post that gives him statewide political leverage." [33] In any event, some observers believe that over the long run, the need for institutions below the national level which are also well-suited to deal with the highest priority domestic problems will prove decisive in favor of the metropolitan government concept.

COUNCIL OF GOVERNMENTS CONCEPT; FEDERAL RULES

Cooperative agreements among local governments are nearly as varied as they are numerous, ranging from a colossus like the Port of New York Authority to a village mosquito control district. The big and the small both have their detractors. William L. Slayton, former U. S. Urban Renewal Commissioner, pointed out to the Senate Subcommittee on Intergovernmental Relations, March 22, 1967:

> We have had sufficient experience with independent, special-purpose authority to realize that it became just that—independent of democratic control and sometimes, unfortunately, the server of special interests. The Washington Suburban Sanitary Commission has had a far greater impact on the way Montgomery County, Md., has developed than has the Maryland National Capital Park and Planning Commission or the Montgomery County Council. Yet it is in no way democratically responsible to the area it serves.

Robert C. Wood has noted that "city hall" in New York, as operator through the New York City Transit Authority of a financially ailing subway system, has fought a long and often losing battle over transportation policy with the Port of New York Authority, which controls vehicular and marine traffic coming into the city from all sides. Commuter railroads, placed in direct competition with the freeway-oriented Port Authority, term the latter the "East India Company" in wry acknowledgment of its favored position.[34]

A newer, and more admired, device to achieve intergov-

---

[33] William Bowen, "Chicago: They Didn't Have to Burn It Down After All," *Fortune*, January 1965, p. 143.
[34] Robert C. Wood, *op. cit.*, p. 137.

ernmental cooperation and research is that of the "council of governments." Starting in the Detroit area 13 years ago, such councils have been formed in the metropolitan areas of Atlanta, Los Angeles, New York, Philadelphia, San Francisco, Seattle-Tacoma, and Washington, D. C. They have been formed also by small and medium-sized cities in Oregon's Willamette Valley.

"The council of governments is so new and unique a concept that any region may make of it what it will," Royce Hanson, president of the Washington Center for Metropolitan Studies, has said. "The council's value depends on the uses to which it is put. . . . Real power in a metropolis comes from the ability to do, not from the opportunity just to know or discuss. Voluntarism is fine, but it is limited." [35]

The federal government took a major step to stimulate metropolitan organization with the Metropolitan Development Act of 1966. It provided that local governments seeking federal grants for certain development projects must have their grants reviewed by metropolitan planning agencies composed "to the greatest practicable extent" of elected local officials. This provision for the first time gave substantive powers to metropolitan planning agencies as well as encouraged the organization of metropolitan government decision-making agencies. More than 36 regional councils have come into being as a result of the requirements of the Act.

---

[35] Royce Hanson, "The Council of Governments: What is it?" *Nation's Cities*, June 1967, p. 7.

PRIVATE ENTERPRISE IN CITY REBUILDING

by

John M. Berry

1 9 6 7
Oct. 4

PRIVATE ENTERPRISE IN CITY REBUILDING

THE JOHNSON ADMINISTRATION has decided to seek help from private enterprise in meeting the urgent requirements of urban slum areas. This is the import of President Johnson's Oct. 2 announcement of a federal test program to attract more private help in creating jobs in areas of hard-core unemployment. Businesses willing to build or expand in a ghetto will find some of their risks reduced by a number of types of government assistance. To succeed, the President said, the venture will require "the concerted action and involvement of the private sector working closely with the federal government."

Riots in a number of cities this past summer make it clear that measures to better the quality of life in slum districts are desperately needed. Yet federal funds are severely limited by the costs of the Viet Nam war—and by the unwillingness of the 90th Congress to step up federal appropriations for antipoverty programs. Under present conditions, the only alternative may be for private business interests to lend a hand on a multi-billion-dollar scale. David Rockefeller, president of the Chase Manhattan Bank, told the Subcommittee on Executive Reorganization of the Senate Government Operations Committee in November 1966 that it was "well to recognize that, in improving our cities, capital investment is needed on an immense scale—an estimated $5 of private capital for each dollar of public funds."

At the same time, Mayor John V. Lindsay of New York City has insisted that no one forget that "We need vigorous national support if we are to redeem the debt the nation has incurred through a century of neglect and oppression."

PROPOSED MASSIVE ATTACK ON URBAN PROBLEMS

Mayor Lindsay had taken a prominent part in a meeting in Washington on Aug. 24 of more than 800 mayors and business, labor, church and civil rights leaders under sponsorship of the Urban Coalition, a national group formed at the end of July to promote "positive and progressive action" on urban problems. The Washington meeting set its sights on a massive attack on slum housing, and on jobs for slum dwellers, by the federal government in conjunction with private enterprise. It declared that the urban crisis required "a new dimension of effort in both the public and private sectors, working together to provide jobs, housing, education, and the other needs of the cities." The meeting called on Congress and the administration, among other things, to take "bold and immediate steps" to get under way a program with "the goal of at least a million housing units for lower-income families annually."

Two days after the meeting in Washington, Gov. Nelson A. Rockefeller of New York said he would ask the legislature to create a New York State Urban Development Corporation to draw private capital into decaying districts. Mayor Lindsay had already announced that he was organizing a New York City unit of the Urban Coalition to bring public and private leaders together to seek solution of the city's problems.

LIFE INSURANCE INVESTMENT IN LOW-COST HOUSING

The life insurance industry, through its Life Insurance Committee on Urban Problems, created by the major companies in May 1967, announced on Sept. 13 that it was prepared to invest $1 billion in slum real estate. The companies plan to divert capital to that purpose, on a pro rata basis, from their normal stream of investments, which is estimated to total about $16 billion a year. When the announcement was made by Gilbert W. Fitzhugh, chairman of the board of the Metropolitan Life Insurance Co., all 348 companies represented on the committee had not indicated whether or not they would participate. However, the two largest— Metropolitan and Prudential—each pledged about $200 million. Most of the initial investments from the fund, which Fitzhugh said would be available immediately, will be in projects whose tenants qualify for rent supplements.[1]

The Prudential Insurance Co. announced, Sept. 21, that it was investing $4.5 million in a new housing project in a Newark district that was ravaged by riots last July. On the

---

[1] The rent supplement program, authorized by Congress in 1965, provides for federal payments to local housing sponsors of that part of a poor tenant's rent that exceeds 25 per cent of his income. The Senate approved on Sept. 19, 1967, the administration's request for $40 million to operate the program in the fiscal year 1968. The House, however, had refused on May 17 to consent to any new appropriation for this purpose. The bill is still in conference.

same day, the White House announced that the life insurance industry had selected eight locations for investments in housing projects: Pittsburgh; Pasco, Wash.; Albuquerque, N.M.; Jacksonville and Lake City, Fla.; Sumter, S.C.; and two sites in Cleveland. President Johnson hailed the move by the life insurance companies as "a historic contribution to our country." *The New Republic,* however, commented on Sept. 30: "On how, precisely, this billion dollars is to be invested, the industry has been vague."

Up to now, the amount of private capital invested in the slums, or available for investment, has been small. Occasional private forays into slum rebuilding have shown that profit in that quarter is generally scant. Historically, profit has been the motivating force behind most private business activity. At the same hearing at which Mayor Lindsay chided the federal government for scrimping on funds for cities, civil rights leader Bayard Rustin said: "David Rockefeller made it very clear to me the other day that the private sector won't provide housing for the hard-core poor and for one simple reason, there is not enough money in it."

There may be some truth in Rustin's statement despite the fact that Rockefeller has long advocated private investment in slum rehabilitation. Experience in renovating slum buildings has shown that, unless rents in the buildings are raised after renovation, the developer has to take a loss. All the signs indicate that private business in general needs not only rent supplements but also tax incentives and other inducements to invest substantial amounts of money in the renewal and rebuilding of central cities.

PLANS TO ATTRACT CAPITAL FOR BUILDING IN SLUMS

Creation by the life insurance companies of a $1 billion investment fund is only one of a number of plans advanced for rebuilding the slums with the help of private funds. Many of the proposed plans would offer inducements to lure private capital into the slums. Sen. Robert F. Kennedy (D N.Y.), for example, has introduced a bill in Congress that would provide tax incentives and low interest rates on mortgages in an effort to promote large-scale private investment in the building and rehabilitation of low-cost rental housing in urban areas.

The major inducement afforded by the Kennedy bill would be a tax credit ranging from 3 per cent on an initial investment of 20 per cent of total project cost up to 22 per cent for a 100 per cent initial investment. The investor would be eligible also for federal mortgage insurance on loans to be made available at below-market interest rates with the government paying the difference. Local governments would be required to limit property taxes to 5 per cent of total rents. In return for these benefits, the sponsor would have to build or rehabilitate at least 100 units of housing for low-income persons only, and agree to retain ownership of and operate the project for no less than 10 years.

Experimental projects involving private enterprise have already been launched in various cities. Small-scale slum renovation programs have been undertaken by the United States Gypsum Co. in the Harlem section of New York and in other cities and by the Armstrong Cork Co. in Philadelphia.[2] In Philadelphia also, Smith, Kline & French, a manufacturer of pharmaceuticals, has subsidized the developers' costs in a 20-block area around its plant, where housing has long been substandard.

In Cleveland, the American Plywood Association, the National Forest Products Association, and the Southern Pine Association are cooperating with a local non-profit organization, Hope Inc. (House Our People Economically), in a plan to rehabilitate frame buildings. Two blocks of three-story detached houses will be converted into A-frame row houses with occasional parks and playgrounds.[3] Warner and Swasey, a heavy equipment and tool manufacturer, has invested more than $100,000 in an apartment building in the riot-scarred Hough section of Cleveland.

PROPOSED PUBLIC FINANCING AND SALE TO INVESTORS

Gov. Rockefeller's state Urban Development Corporation was first projected, in 1966, on a national scale. The Department of Housing and Urban Development and the White House Office of Science and Technology sponsored a science and urban development conference that summer at Woods Hole, Mass., that proposed such a corporation. But the necessary legislation was never introduced.

The corporation proposed by the New York governor would initiate and in some cases construct slum area projects that would include not only housing but also facilities

---

[2] See p. 729.

[3] "Big Business Corporations Are Becoming Involved in Urban Rehabilitation," *Journal of Housing,* May 1967, pp. 211-216.

for light industry, stores, and other small business enterprises. The projects, if not built by private interests, would be sold to them after completion. Rockefeller said he would ask the New York legislature to appropriate $50 million to launch the corporation, which would thereafter finance itself by issuing revenue bonds and relying on existing state programs for "seed" money.

Some observers think that President Johnson may propose early next year a similar program to get more private money into the slums. Gov. Rockefeller having adopted the plan suggested by the Woods Hole conference, the President is said to need a new idea:

> The essential concept [of Rockefeller's plan] is Hortense Gabel's, former commissioner of rent and rehabilitation in New York City. . . . Johnson must now rely on his Kaiser Commission to develop a program sufficiently original to differentiate it from the Rockefeller program. This would be a good trick, because Miss Gabel also helped to design Johnson's original program.[4]

The Kaiser Commission, a special presidential commission on urban housing headed by industrialist Edgar Kaiser, was set up in April 1967 to devise ways of luring private capital into the low-income housing field. It has come up with only one recommendation so far. It suggested on Aug. 17 that the Department of Housing and Urban Development undertake a pilot program involving private developers in not only the construction but also the management of public housing. Such a program would be, in effect, an extension of the present "turnkey" approach, under which a developer comes to the housing authority with a site and plans and the authority agrees to buy the finished product at a fixed price. The Kaiser Commission is expected to make further proposals in December.

In the meantime, the administration has been critical of some of the approaches to joint private and government attacks on slums problems. Discussing the Urban Coalition's proposals at a news conference on Aug. 25, Housing and Urban Development Secretary Robert C. Weaver suggested that Congress and the American people, not the administration, lacked a sense of urgency about slum problems. Weaver reminded reporters that the President had "repeatedly urged Congress to pass urban aid programs totaling $6 billion."

President Johnson has said that he will devote his efforts

---

[4] Michael Miles, "The Politics of Consortium," *New Republic*, Sept. 9, 1967, pp. 11-13.

now to getting through Congress the appropriations necessary for existing programs. Both rent supplements and the model cities program—a comprehensive plan for rebuilding entire neighborhoods through a combination of federal aid, local cooperation, and private capital—have suffered fund cuts.

PUBLIC LAND FOR PRIVATELY FINANCED MODEL CITIES

One new federal plan to help meet the urban crisis—the use of federal land for "model communities"—has been advanced by the administration. President Johnson disclosed, Aug. 30, that a privately financed community for about 25,000 persons would be built on a 335-acre plot of federal land in the District of Columbia. The federal government is to make available without charge the land on which low-income housing will be constructed, and it will either lease or sell the remaining land for construction of moderately priced dwellings and commercial facilities. The intention is to enable the developer, who will also operate the housing, to make a profit on units for low-income families as well as on other dwellings.

"This new venture," the President said, "will be first and foremost a partnership—a partnership between local and federal governments, private developers and the people of the city." He ordered a survey of other available federal properties to see if any could be used for similar projects.

Private Experiments in Urban Renewal

THE CRISIS of the central city is not new. With their middle-class residents moving out and their tax bases eroding, central cities have been in trouble for years. Recent riots have underscored the magnitude of that trouble. Today, three out of four Americans live in urban centers. Within the next two decades, the proportion is expected to reach four out of five.

Beginning with the Housing Act of 1937, Congress has put on the books a series of laws aimed to improve the quality of urban life. The first instrument selected to cope with slums was public housing. It soon became apparent that it provided only a limited answer to the question of how to house people with lower-than-average incomes.

The Housing Act of 1949 incorporated the concept of urban redevelopment—that is, the clearing of deteriorated urban areas and reuse of the land. The act stated that "Private enterprise should be encouraged to serve as large a part of the total needs as it can." Government aid was intended to spur private enterprise to meet more of the housing need. Local public bodies were expected to sponsor programs for better neighborhoods at lower costs through the medium of the "entrepreneur-builder." Finally, public agencies were to sponsor low-income housing only where private efforts were insufficient.

The act called for public acquisition of land—by negotiation or condemnation—and resale of the land to a private developer at a "fair value" appropriate to its reuse, *i.e.* at a reduced price. "Not since the building of the railroads in the West a full century before had the United States government devised a program aimed specifically, as was Title I of the Housing Act of 1949, at involving private enterprise in a peacetime public purpose." [5]

By 1954, only 60 of the 211 localities which had expressed interest in urban redevelopment had reached the land acquisition stage. Of $500 million available in grants, only $74 million had been committed. That year Congress passed a third and broader housing act. Under the 1954 act, cities applying for federal money were required to submit a "workable program," a comprehensive city-wide plan for slum clearance and prevention. As one writer described it:

> Once the city presented its workable program, all of the federal aids, new and old, would become available. The private builders would, as before, be the main functionaries in the urban renewal performance, and they could have either cleared sites turned over to them for new building or they might have FHA-insured financing for rehabilitation of old ones.[6]

Private enterprise nevertheless made a cautious debut on the urban renewal scene. By January 1960, only 26 of 699 approved projects had been completed.

LESSONS IN STUYVESANT TOWN AND OTHER PROJECTS

There were virtually no attempts at city redevelopment by private groups before 1949. An exception was the Metro-

---

[5] Jeanne R. Lowe, *Cities in a Race With Time* (1967), p. 68.
[6] Charles Abrams, *The City is the Frontier* (1965), p. 87.

politan Life Insurance Co.'s Stuyvesant Town project in New York City. Park Commissioner Robert Moses had induced the company in 1943 to try its hand at redeveloping an 18-block area on the Lower East Side. Stuyvesant Town differed from urban renewal projects in that neither federal assistance nor a write-down on land cost was involved. The company agreed to limit its profit to 6 per cent. The buildings were to be exempt from real estate taxes, which, combined with limited dividends, was supposed to result in low rents and a safe investment.

Although the rents were low, tenants did not have to be from low-income groups. At first, Metropolitan had refused to rent to Negroes and, in fact, won court sanction for that policy, but a local law soon made such discrimination illegal. After the racial discrimination suit and a tenant protest against a rent increase, the company decided to undertake no more such projects. Stuyvesant Town nevertheless had demonstrated "that the presence of qualified Negroes in a project does not drive out the white tenants or endanger the company's investment [and] that urban renewal schemes are sound in sound cities and can be rentable and profitable investments for the big capital pools when the city assembles the land and clears the site." [7]

Later private ventures into the slums have brought to light some of the problems which may arise. In 1962 New York's Citizens' Housing and Planning Council, a private non-profit civic organization using private money, renovated a six-story apartment building on which it hoped to make a profit sufficient to demonstrate the value of such investments and attract other private investors into the field. The council found only that the "property might have returned a reasonable profit if it had been possible to (a) charge higher rents or (b) keep the total development cost down or (c) reduce operating expenses or (d) do all three." [8] It had to conclude that none of these things was possible and that the project had not been a success.

Rental and Management Associates inherited by judicial mandate in July 1965 seven decaying East Harlem buildings that had accumulated more than 600 housing code violations. The group tried to fix up the buildings, but the income from

---

[7] *Ibid.,* pp. 97-98.
[8] "Old Building & Low-Income Tenants & Profit-Seeking Rehabilitation," *Journal of Housing,* January 1967, p. 32.

rents was insufficient to pay the bill for repairs. It was decided in the end that the only hope for the buildings and the tenants was rehabilitation by a non-profit organization.[9]

On a larger scale, there is the experience of the Aluminum Company of America. Alcoa was drawn into two major real estate ventures in New York and Los Angeles by developer William Zeckendorf. It also bought substantial interests in eight other renewal projects in New York, Pittsburgh, Philadelphia and San Francisco. By 1964, the company was ready to quit. It listed rent ceilings, high city taxes, proximity of slums, F.H.A. delays, and local bureaucracy as some of its problems. Alcoa decided that traditional private financing was simpler than dealing with a government mortgage.[10] Recently, however, Alcoa was one of six companies which pledged funds to the Allegheny Housing Corporation whose goal is to build 1,000 units of low-cost housing a year for five years in the Pittsburgh area.[11]

POSSIBILITIES IN ADVANCED CONSTRUCTION TECHNIQUES

Some people believe that private ventures into slum rebuilding and rehabilitation could be made more successful if costs were reduced by greater resort to modern technology. One of the most dramatic demonstrations of new methods was given recently by a project financed by HUD— the much-publicized 48-hour "Instant Rehabilitation" on the Lower East Side of New York. At least 10 private manufacturers of building supplies developed the products used in the demonstration. The purpose was to show what the private building industry could do—granting modification of union rules and revision of antiquated building codes—if it updated its methods.

Using a "systems approach" developed by Conrad Engineers, an old building was rapidly gutted and core units (kitchens, bathrooms, etc.) were lowered into place to be installed by teams of technicians working in shifts. HUD estimated that it had shaved $2,000 per apartment off the cost of rehabilitation by using the new techniques. If new techniques were applied to a number of buildings, the savings would be even greater, particularly in New York where

---

[9] Philip Schorr, "Only as Much as the Rents Will Bear," *Journal of Housing*, January 1967, pp. 33-36.

[10] See Leon E. Hickman (executive vice president, Alcoa), "Alcoa's Renewal Role Explained", *Journal of Housing*, May 1964, pp. 190-195.

[11] See p. 730.

there are about 57,000 tenements of more or less standard design.[12]

The systems approach to housing is an outgrowth of the 1966 Woods Hole conference, whose report pointed out the success that the National Aeronautics and Space Administration had had in integrating "the efforts of government, universities and industry to put our country into the race to the moon." After it had been shown what innovations were needed to provide spacecraft, "ways were found to bring them about." [13]

An example of the systems approach is a consortium now being formed by Gen. Bernard A. Schriever (U.S.A.F. ret.), architect of the Air Force's ballistic missile program. The Schriever consortium, which is still in the planning stages, may be called Urban Inc. Roughly 11 companies in the engineering, construction, architectural and transportation fields would supply the capital and know-how for what is intended to be a profit-making venture. To date, several aerospace companies have expressed interest.

Some advanced technology has been available to the building trades for years. The germ of the idea for inserting core elements into an old building can be found in the revolutionary work of the designer-architect, Buckminister Fuller. Fuller invented precast units in the 1930s, but they were never accepted. He is the inventor also of various kinds of prefabricated, easily transported houses and of geodesic domes. The domes, though widely used by the armed forces, were designed primarily to provide inexpensive, durable housing.[14]

A young architect, Moshe Safdie, who says that Fuller has greatly influenced his thinking, designed for Canada's Expo 67 the extraordinary apartment house called Habitat 67. It consists of reinforced concrete boxes that were prefabricated on the ground and lifted into place by a giant crane. The units are held together by cables. Any number of concrete dwelling units can be attached, and each provides privacy, a sheltered terrace and sunlight. Habitat 67 was expensive to build because of the cost of the machinery

---

[12] "Big Business Corporations Are Becoming Involved in Urban Rehabilitation," *Journal of Housing*, May 1967, pp. 211-216.

[13] U. S. Department of Housing and Urban Development, *Science and the City*, January 1967, p. 6.

[14] See Buckminister Fuller, *Ideas and Integrities, A Spontaneous Autobiographical Disclosure* (1963). A geodesic dome houses the U. S. exhibition at Canada's Expo 67 in Montreal.

for making and raising the concrete units relative to the number built. But if enough dwelling units were constructed, the cost per unit might be very low.[15]

VENTURES IN PRIVATE REBUILDING OF SLUM HOUSING

The activity in Harlem of United States Gypsum, a building materials manufacturer, is often cited as a successful example of private enterprise at work in the slums. The company started with deteriorated but basically sound six-story tenements and is renovating them. The first building was completed and reoccupied by its former tenants in January 1967. However, rents were raised from $28 to $78 an apartment. The difference was partly subsidized by a $76,000 low-income housing demonstration grant from HUD. United States Gypsum thinks that the present rents are sufficient to keep the building in good shape and to pay off the mortgage. It has plans for similar renovation in other cities and has invested more than $1 million in demonstration projects. The company says it "is attempting to prove to private enterprise that blighted and run-down buildings can be profitably restored for decent family living, in full compliance with codes." [16]

Armstrong Cork Co., also a manufacturer of building products, rehabilitated a Philadelphia brick row house recently and has announced plans to undertake the rehabilitation of seven row houses in Lancaster, Pa., its headquarters. In four months, Armstrong converted the Philadelphia house into a three-family apartment building, using its own products wherever possible.

John R. Baldwin, Armstrong's manager of contract market development, said of the Philadelphia project: "This test project in Philadelphia was undertaken to try to find answers to some of the difficult problems in urban rehabilitation. As we see them, these problems include available financing plans, contracting, new product development, new ways of installing materials more quickly and more easily and learning the profit potential for private industry—manufacturer, builder-remodeler, and subcontractor." [17]

---

[15] HUD has asked Safdie to submit a design for an unspecified project, possibly the low-income housing project to be built in Washington on land donated by the federal government. This is the first time that HUD has sought revolutionary design in a low-income housing unit.

[16] Douglas Cray, "Business Puts Its Focus on Problems of Slums," *New York Times*, Sept. 3, 1967, p. F1.

[17] *Ibid.*, p. 212.

In some cities, groups of business men have been conspicuously successful in getting things done. The classic example is Pittsburgh, where the Allegheny Conference was formed in 1943 by Richard K. Mellon. The conference included many other wealthy men, heads of giant corporations, and city officials. Starting with a park, new bridges and a smoke control ordinance, the coalition gradually revived the center of the city. The difficult matter of housing got shelved, however, until 1956 when ACTION-Housing Inc. (Allegheny Council to Improve Our Neighborhoods) was formed.

After more than 10 years, ACTION-Housing is finally beginning to show results. One reason for the delay has been cited by Jeanne Lowe:

> In the shelter field . . . Pittsburghers were not yet willing to consider public means for reducing shelter costs for the "forgotten third." New York, with its municipal tax abatement and low-interest government loans, was able to do much more, proportionately, than did ACTION-Housing. The necessary enabling legislation was said to be politically impossible.[18]

Recently ACTION-Housing has undertaken what it calls "a deeply researched proposal aimed at a breakthrough in housing rehabilitation." It acquired 22 row houses and remodeled them for about $299,000. Its executive director, Bernard E. Loshbough, said that this project was economically feasible because, as a non-profit organization, ACTION-Housing was able to obtain below-market 3 per cent interest money under the National Housing Act. It also had a development fund, an interest-bearing revolving loan.

Similar projects would be feasible throughout the country, Loshbough said, "if a group of large companies, either allied with the building industry or interested in revitalizing aging neighborhoods, form and manage a limited-profit development corporation for the rehabilitation of housing, in cooperation with appropriate public agencies." He added that "Such a corporation should be allied with a non-profit research company, which would sponsor research in construction methods and work with material application problems requiring solution."[19] An organization of the type outlined, the Allegheny Housing Corporation, is slowly taking shape in Pittsburgh.

---

[18] Jeanne R. Lowe, *op. cit.*, p. 161.

[19] Bernard E. Loshbough, "Pittsburgh Renovates 22 Houses in Aging Neighborhood to Demonstrate Effectiveness of Combined Private Enterprise and Government as a Rehabilitation Team," *Journal of Housing*, May 1967, p. 210.

Schemes to Boost New Jobs and Business

SLUMS, increasingly the scene of riots, are considered poor locations for business and employment centers. In the Watts district of Los Angeles, 40 stores and other business establishments were destroyed in six days of rioting in 1965. Only three were rebuilt, although five new businesses have opened there more recently. Aerojet General Corp., a California company, built a plant in Watts in January 1967 and then looked for something it could make. The enterprise, called the Watts Manufacturing Co., now employs about 200 local residents, at average hourly pay of $2.08, to make tents for the armed forces.

This experience has been cited as demonstrating that hard-core unemployed may become employable if they feel they are wanted; that on-the-job training for such persons is feasible if they have an incentive; that police records make no difference (the pilferage rate in the Watts plant has been lower than at some companies where a police record is a bar to employment); and that private enterprise can bring jobs to the disadvantaged although it needs a boost from the government to do so.

An "Urban Plant Investment" bill, introduced in the Senate by Sen. Robert F. Kennedy, aims to provide the needed boost. It would encourage corporations to locate plants in slum areas by giving them a 10 per cent federal tax credit, accelerated depreciation of the plants, and other tax benefits. To qualify for the benefits, the company would have to create at least 50 new jobs and fill two-thirds of them with persons living in the slum area.

Other more limited approaches tried by some corporations include various forms of on-the-job training and special attempts to hire slum residents. Several years ago, the McDonnell Douglas Corp. launched a program in St. Louis to hire and train the disadvantaged. The drawback in this case was that the McDonnell plant was 12 miles and a long bus trip away from the city's slums.[20]

Another company, Corn Products, finding itself unable to fill many jobs because numerous job applicants and a good

[20] Alfonso J. Cervantes (Mayor of St. Louis), "To Prevent a Chain of Super-Watts," *Harvard Business Review*, September-October 1967, pp. 55-65.

number of its own lower-level employees were functionally illiterate, decided to teach its workers the basic literacy skills at its own expense. Last autumn it gave 38 workers, at a cost of $400 each, enough instruction to pass a qualifying examination for promotion. Eastman Kodak has called in the Board for Fundamental Education, an organization chartered by Congress that has been working on problems of this sort for 30 years, to do the same kind of thing.[21]

BUSINESS FINANCING IN HARLEM; JAVITS' BANK PLAN

The paucity of business enterprises, large or small, in slum areas poses an acute problem. In Harlem today, there are only 2,400 business establishments, most of them small and owned by whites. Small slum businesses have many problems, including financing and high insurance rates, which would not plague larger businesses operating in the same districts. Traditional financing is often unavailable to the slum resident who would like to start a business.

Three Harlem businessmen who organized the Trans Urban Construction Co. in 1964 and did $1.5 million worth of business in 1966 afford an exception to the general rule. One of them told reporters that it was fairly easy to set up small retail and service businesses. The hard thing was to get the financing and the able management needed to establish a productive business like construction or manufacturing.

To get its own financing, Trans Urban founded the Freedom National Bank, in some ways the most important business in Harlem. It is already the largest Negro bank in the United States. Freedom National often will lend money when Harlem branches of downtown banks will not. However, because of limited assets, it cannot make a loan of more than $110,000.

Situations like that found in Harlem inspired Sen. Jacob K. Javits (R N.Y.) to propose establishment of a "domestic development bank" patterned after the World Bank. The bank would be designed to make long-term, low-interest mortgage loans to businesses in high-risk areas. Javits suggests that it be authorized to raise up to $10 billion through sales of stock or bonds. The loans it makes might cover up to 90 per cent of the cost of establishing a business enter-

---

[21] Rasa Gustaitis, "Private Industry's Factory Classrooms," *The Reporter*, Sept. 7, 1967, pp. 23-24.

prise, bear interest at about 7 per cent, and be repayable in 30 years. A companion proposal would provide for creation of an "Economic and Social Opportunity Corporation" to supply technical assistance and do research for businesses seeking to locate in the slums.

This approach differs sharply from that of the Kennedy plan to provide tax incentives for businesses that locate in slum areas. The Kennedy plan is geared to appeal to big corporations but would be of little help to a small business-man starting from scratch.

A plan to enlist private enterprise in slum revitalization was launched in January 1967 in Brooklyn's Bedford-Stuy-vesant section. The plan, initiated by Sen. Robert F. Ken-nedy, provides what is in effect a partnership between private enterprise, government and the community. The Bedford-Stuyvesant Development and Services Corp. was formed to stimulate investment in the Brooklyn slum. Members of the consortium offer financial backing to any resident who presents a feasible plan for starting a busi-ness there.

The Kennedy plan attempts to involve the people of the area in planning through a community corporation called the Bedford-Stuyvesant Restoration Corp. As might be expected, this has been where most of the problems have arisen as local factions fought among themselves for power. In fact, this dissension has largely prevented the project from moving out of the planning stages to date.

PLANS TO FOSTER HOME OWNERSHIP IN CITY SLUMS

Home ownership is another promising area involving private enterprise, in this case the slum dweller himself. The experience of the Bicentennial Civic Improvement Corp. in St. Louis, a non-profit neighborhood organization, has shown that the slum dweller's interest in his environment changes when he owns a house. B.C.I.C. has been buying houses cheaply (it acknowledges that its ability to do so is one of the reasons for its success), renovating them and selling them for $6,500 to $7,000 on 100 per cent loans.

In order to create a 100 per cent loan, B.C.I.C. has deposited the 20 per cent down payment, due to itself as seller, in a savings account with the [financing savings and loan] association, to be held as security until 20 per cent of the 100 per cent is paid off. The money for these security deposits was borrowed from a downtown bank. The down payments have thus cost B.C.I.C. the difference between their borrowing cost downtown and the interest their security deposits earn.[22]

By May 1967, 62 families had acquired homes, and B.C.I.C. had found that incomes were apt to rise when a family lives in a house it owns. Also, home ownership appears to be an antidote to the problems of vandalism and neglect that are typical of both low-income housing projects and slums.

Home ownership depends upon the availability of mortgage financing, and for most slum dwellers it has not been available. A "Home Ownership Foundation" bill, introduced in the Senate by Sen. Charles H. Percy (R Ill.), seems to tackle the problem, but it is aimed at lower-middle income families, not those at the bottom of the heap. Sen. Percy has described his bill as follows:

> The National Home Ownership Foundation would have two essential functions: (1) to provide the needed technical know-how and expertise to local groups sponsoring home ownership programs for lower income families who have, or can develop, the potential for carrying a modest mortgage, and (2) to make mortgage funds available to finance projects which do not now have direct access to local capital.[23]

At the heart of the proposal is a federal guarantee of principal and interest on up to $2 million in debentures to be issued by the foundation and an interest subsidy to be paid by the U. S. Treasury to reduce monthly payments on individual mortgages. On April 21, Secretary Weaver issued an analysis of the Percy plan which said it was "well-intentioned" but indicated "little real understanding of the problems of producing housing within the economic means of poor people." Most urban poor, Weaver said, do not have stable enough incomes to take advantage of the plan.

It was reported on Sept. 28 that a bipartisan plan to promote home ownership for slum families had been worked out after weeks of private negotiations between Senators Percy and Walter F. Mondale (D Minn.), both members of the Senate Banking and Currency Committee. Under the compromise, a National Home Ownership Foundation would

[22] Michael J. Mazer and Richard S. Granat, "St. Louis Combines Nonprofit Rehabilitation Financing with Community Organization and Social Services to Bring Home Ownership to Low-Income Families," *Journal of Housing*, May 1967, p. 201.

[23] Sen. Charles H. Percy, "National Home Ownership Foundation—Mortgages for the Poor," *The Mortgage Banker*, July 1967.

still be set up, but its role would be much more limited. It would provide technical assistance and, in some cases, seed money to local groups. Maximum incomes for eligible families would be pegged at 70 per cent of the income requirements now in force for the federal government's so-called "moderate income" housing program. This would mean a maximum income for a family of five of $6,755 in the District of Columbia, $4,935 in Birmingham, Ala., and $7,035 in Chicago and New York. Private banks would make and service the low-interest loans, which would be government insured.

NEED FOR BETTER GOVERNMENT-BUSINESS COOPERATION

It has been noted that none of the plans now before the Congress would directly help the poorest segment of slum dwellers—the 32 million Americans, or one person in every six, who live in families where the breadwinner is unemployed, on welfare or whose income hovers at or slightly above minimum wage levels. In these cases, private capital's involvement is viewed as no substitute for public housing.

Yet some kind of cooperation between government and private enterprise will be necessary for a true renaissance in the nation's urban centers. St. Louis mayor Alfonso J. Cervantes recently wrote that "Ultimately it must be private industry that figures out ways to integrate the disadvantaged—especially the Negro—into the economy and to dissolve the slum, or it will soon be necessary to despair not only of the slums but of the total central city. Either businessmen will learn new techniques of job simplification, personnel management, and skill development and take over the leadership of the thrust against chronic unemployment, or it will be necessary to withdraw from the central city and seal it off as the leprous Pandora's box of American society." [24]

[24] Alfonso J. Cervantes, "To Prevent a Chain of Super-Watts," *Harvard Business Review*, September-October 1967, pp. 55-65.

WELFARE REFORMS

by

Helen B. Shaffer

1 9 6 7
Dec. 20

WELFARE REFORMS

CONTROVERSY over welfare policy, stirred up by sharp differences on the proper way to handle what may be described as a welfare crisis, is likely to be intensified rather than stilled by the outcome of a bitter contest on the question between House and Senate. Major changes in federal welfare law—included in the conference agreement on the 1967 Amendments to the Social Security Act—were effected only by capitulation of the Senate to House demands.[1] And the signs are that the matter will not be allowed to rest there.

The depth of the difference in outlook between the two houses, which reflected a comparable division in the population, was revealed when details of the conference report became known on Dec. 8. Six senators,[2] including three members of the Finance Committee which had prepared the version of the measure originally approved by the Senate, assailed the conference compromise for its harsh and "regressive" provisions on public assistance to welfare recipients. Several of the protesting senators felt that the provisions were so damaging that the entire bill should be held over for reconsideration when Congress reconvened for its second session, Jan. 15, 1968.

Two provisions of the conference agreement raised particular objection: (1) the imposition of a ceiling on the number of children for whom the federal government would provide matching funds under the program for Aid to Families with Dependent Children, the limit being set at the percentage of children in each state on relief rolls on Jan. 1, 1968; and (2) a job training and employment requirement which critics said would virtually force the mothers of dependent children to take low-paying, menial jobs while leav-

[1] The conference report was agreed to by the House by a vote of 288-3 on Dec. 13, and by the Senate, by a vote of 62-14 on Dec. 15.

[2] The protesting senators, all Democrats, were Fred R. Harris (Okla.), Vance Hartke (Ind.), Robert F. Kennedy (N.Y.), Lee Metcalf (Mont.), Walter F. Mondale (Minn.), and Wayne Morse (Ore.).

ing their young children under institutional care. Sen. Robert F. Kennedy (D N.Y.) called the welfare section of the bill "one of the most regressive pieces of legislation ever to emerge from a House-Senate conference, . . . a disgrace to all Americans, and an affront to . . . the poor."

The issue is certain to be raised again early in the new session. The liberal group, led by Sen. Fred R. Harris (D Okla.), intends to introduce new amendments to remove the offending provisions of the 1967 act. The White House has promised its support of this move.

It was clear that the dominant mood of Congress in relation to Public Assistance was impatience over its growth—most particularly the increasing number of persons on A.F.D.C. rolls, a contingent made up chiefly of husbandless women and their minor children. The attitude of Congress was strongly influenced by complaints of constituents resentful of the obligation imposed on taxpayers to support families of able-bodied but non-working parents, or of parents who evade their responsibilities by deserting. Fiscal problems of the big cities, brought on by the mounting cost of providing municipal services, also bore on the determination of Congress somehow to cut rising welfare expenditures. Considerations of federal budget-balancing, in view of the drain on tax funds caused by the war in Viet Nam, were of course paramount.

CONNECTION BETWEEN WELFARE AND URBAN TENSION

Another element made itself felt as congressional committees weighed various proposals for reducing the welfare burden. In the background they heard the swelling voices of an increasingly aggressive and articulate "community of the poor," demanding more aid, not as a bounty but as a "right." Congress has amended welfare law many times since the present system was established under the Social Security Act of 1935. But never before has it worked on important revisions in an atmosphere of such tension over the failures and shortcomings of the basic poor-aid system. The reason is obvious: welfare has become deeply enmeshed in some of the most complex and socially disruptive situations the nation has ever faced. Almost the entire gamut of urban problems, from street crime to inadequate tax revenue, is involved.

Welfare Reforms

SIGNIFICANT FACTS ABOUT PUBLIC ASSISTANCE

	September 1966	September 1967
Number of persons receiving assistance:		
Old Age Assistance	2,084,000	2,065,000
Aid to the Blind	84,400	82,800
Aid to Permanently and Totally Disabled	580,000	629,000
Aid to Families with Dependent Children	4,508,000	5,102,000
General Assistance (non-federal aid)	597,000	729,000
Total Recipients of Money Payments..	7,853,400	8,607,800
Total Expenditures for Public Assistance, federal, state, and local, for one month..	$535,603,000	$673,218,000

The welfare crisis is an important facet of the Negro protest. Anger of the ghetto poor at "the establishment" has often found its nearest target in the local welfare office. "Poverty and race are profoundly entangled in America," a critic of the system has written; public assistance has been "a means . . . of underwriting and institutionalizing urban poverty associated specifically with de facto segregation in the North." [3]

The link between welfare policy and the tinderbox situation in the city ghettos is widely recognized. "Affluence and poverty are on a collision course in America today," a high-ranking federal welfare official told a convention of the American Public Welfare Association on Dec. 8, "and the time to act is short." [4] A director of the National Welfare Rights Organization, representing the poor on relief, told the same gathering that the "welfare establishment" bore "heavy responsibility for rioting and rebellion."

A.F.L.-C.I.O. President George R. Meany was one of a number of witnesses before the Senate Finance Committee who cited the urban crisis-welfare link when urging modification of some of the harsher welfare provisions of the Social Security bill approved by the House. "Our welfare system," he said on Sept. 19, "deeply affects the mood and temper of the slums."

[3] William Stringfellow, "The Representation of the Poor in American Society," *Law and Contemporary Problems*, Winter 1966, p. 143.
[4] Mary E. Switzer, Commissioner of the Vocational Rehabilitation Administration, U.S. Department of Health, Education, and Welfare.

Concern over last summer's riots and the threat of more and worse disorders in the months ahead have been cited to explain why the business community is showing an interest in welfare policy that goes beyond the question of its cost to the taxpayer. This point was made by several observers when the Business Council, a group of top executives which advises the government on policies affecting business, broke precedent by devoting a session of its autumn meeting to social welfare questions. Among those who addressed the council was the New York City welfare commissioner, Mitchell L. Ginsberg, a severe critic of the present poor-aid system and a proponent of a child-and-family allowance plan.[5]

WORRY IN CONGRESS ABOUT RISING WELFARE COSTS

Public welfare has long been under fire from both the providers and the recipients of its benefits. Mayor John V. Lindsay of New York City, testifying before the Senate Finance Committee, Sept. 12, 1967, referred to the 32-year-old system as "in many ways . . . a philosophic and financial flop." Lindsay's welfare commissioner described the system as "bankrupt," overdue for discarding. After completing field studies of a number of local poverty programs in the Middle Atlantic region, consultants to another Senate committee reported:

> In all of the communities studied, there is profound hostility, suspicion and damning criticism of public welfare, . . . its rules, regulations . . . and its income standards. This agency catches it from both sides: the affluent damn it because it pauperizes the poor at their expense; the poor damn it because it demands a demeaning attitude from them.[6]

Commissioner Mary E. Switzer of the U.S. Vocational Rehabilitation Administration told the American Public Welfare Association, Dec. 8, that the prevailing attitude toward public welfare was due to "the frustration that comes from a seemingly uncontrollable rise in aid costs without an accompanying effort to reduce the relief load by alternate ways of dealing with the problem of need."

The House Ways and Means Committee, in reporting out the bill which was to become, with relatively few changes,

[5] Ginsberg, now New York City's Human Resources Administrator, spoke at a Business Council session at Hot Springs, Va., Oct. 21, 1967.

[6] Subcommittee on Employment, Manpower, and Poverty of Senate Committee on Labor and Public Welfare, *Examination of the War on Poverty: Staff and Consultants' Reports*, Vol. V, September 1967, p. 1242.

the Social Security Amendments of 1967, explained why it included drastic provisions aimed to hold down the number of welfare recipients—provisions critics had labeled "punitive" toward children of the poor:

> Your committee is very deeply concerned that such a large number of families have not achieved independence and self-support, and is very greatly concerned over the rapidly increasing costs to the taxpayers. Moreover, your committee is aware that the growth in this program has received increasingly critical attention.[7]

"We are rough in this bill," Chairman Wilbur D. Mills said. "We intend to be—but we do not intend to be inhuman."

Though the Senate deleted some of the harsher features of the House bill before passing its version on Nov. 22, there was little difference between the two houses in the nature of their concern over the welfare problem. "Like the Committee on Ways and Means . . .," the Senate Finance Committee said in its report, "this committee has become concerned about the continued growth in the number of [A.F.D.C.] families." It too was "very greatly concerned over the rapidly increasing costs to the taxpayers" and was "aware" of the "increasingly critical public attention" directed to the welfare system.[8]

EXERTION OF PRESSURE BY MOTHERS ON WELFARE

Meanwhile, new pressures for change of a different sort were rising from the ranks of the poor and their spokesmen. Grievances of welfare recipients against public assistance are as old as the system itself. The significant new element is the banding together of welfare clients to press for redress of their grievances, and the use of tactics of social action comparable to those employed in agitation for civil rights. In city after city, mothers on A.F.D.C. rolls have formed such groups as MAW (Mothers for Adequate Welfare, in Boston), MOM (Mothers' Organized Movement, in Wichita), CUFAW (Citizens United For Adequate Welfare, in Cleveland) and others. Groups of this kind have had some success in their localities in obtaining more out of the welfare system than might otherwise have come their way.

Such local activity led to the formation in June 1967 of the National Welfare Rights Organization, the first national

---

[7] House Committee on Ways and Means, *Social Security Amendments of 1967*, Aug. 7, 1967, pp. 95-96.
[8] Senate Finance Committee, *Social Security Amendments of 1967*, Nov. 14, 1967, p. 145.

organization of recipients or potential recipients of public assistance. According to George A. Wiley, director of the Poverty Rights Action Center in Washington, D. C., where N.W.R.O. has its headquarters, the new organization has 4,000 dues-paying members representing 15,000 welfare recipients directly, and "indirectly more than five million [A.F.D.C.] mothers and their children." [9]

The organization held its first convention, in Washington, on Aug. 28, drawing an estimated 1,000 delegates from 50 or more cities. The day's events included a rally on Capitol Hill at which speakers denounced the then-pending public assistance bill as a "betrayal of the poor"; a "mothers' march" on the Department of Health, Education, and Welfare, where the women sought unsuccessfully to meet with H.E.W. Secretary John W. Gardner; and a mock hearing at the Capitol to protest the Senate Finance Committee's refusal to hear testimony from the women that day.

Officers of the new organization were not appeased when they received permission to testify before the committee later. "We wanted to be heard by the committee when all . . . of the delegates from . . . 22 states . . . [were] in town," Wiley told the committee on Sept. 19 before turning over most of his allotted time to the welfare mothers accompanying him. The women not only criticized the aid system but also commented sharply on the "empty seats" of committee members.

"Since we suffered so hard and begged and borrowed money and gas and drivers . . . to get here," one of the women said, more than one or two members should have been present to listen to them. Other witnesses spoke in more threatening terms. One mother said: "You think you had trouble this summer. . . . There is going to come a time when the fire starts burning and your children are going to suffer. . . . So take your heads out of the sand."

When the committee recessed at noon, the welfare delegation expected to resume testifying at an afternoon session. However, Finance Committee Chairman Russell B. Long (D La.) returned in the afternoon only to adjourn the hearing. Because the women refused to leave for a time after that, the episode was dubbed a welfare sit-in. Neither testimony nor the sit-in had apparent effect on the committee's action. But they did point up the gap of understanding and sym-

---

[9] Testimony, Senate Finance Committee, Sept. 19, 1967.

pathy between those who suspect public welfare of harboring parasites and cheaters and those who believe that public welfare punishes the unfortunate for the "crime" of being poor. Chairman Long described the welfare witnesses the next day as "a group of people speaking for welfare persons who are not working and do not want to work." He added: "If they can find time to march in the streets and . . . picket congressional committees, and . . . to sit all day in committee hearings . . ., [they] should have time to do some work."

Grievances Against Public Assistance

THE WELFARE PROTEST movement is a byproduct of the recent emergence of the very poor (especially the Negro poor of the urban ghetto) from political quiescence. No longer silent and no longer "invisible" to the middle-class majority, the poorest of the poor are making an unprecedented effort to exert influence over policies governing public programs that directly affect their daily lives.

The anti-poverty program developed under the Economic Opportunity Act of 1964, while separate from the operations of Public Assistance, nevertheless has played an important role in the growth of the new challenge to the welfare system. A major goal of the Economic Opportunity Act was to overcome inertia among the long-time poor; to stir hope in them of bettering their condition, and to help them find ways to participate in the normal processes of a democratic society.

The Community Action phase of the program has been the chief instrument for carrying out the statutory mandate that the poor participate in running programs affecting their personal lives and their communities. "Through Community Action," stated a poverty agency report, "the poor have found their voice." [10] In a number of cases, this voice has been directed to the local welfare agency and has resulted in new tensions between welfare clients and established welfare agencies unaccustomed to having their decisions challenged by the beneficiaries of welfare.[11]

[10] U.S. Office of Economic Opportunity, *The Quiet Revolution.*
[11] The influence of Community Action in this respect may be watered down as a result of a provision in the Economic Opportunity Act of 1967 giving greater control of poverty activities to established agencies of local government.

The anti-poverty program has spurred the poor to battle for their welfare "rights" in two ways: it has informed them of rights they possess of which many were ignorant— the right, for example, to appeal an unfavorable ruling— and it has provided legal counsel to help the poor present their cases before the welfare agencies or to the courts.

GROWTH OF LITIGATION IN THE FIELD OF WELFARE

There never has been such a time of litigation on welfare issues. Hundreds of O.E.O.-sponsored Neighborhood Legal Service centers for the poor have been established. In addition, such older legal organizations concerned with civil rights as the Legal Defense Fund of the National Association for the Advancement of Colored People and the American Civil Liberties Union have become more active in the welfare field than in the past.

The Center on Social Welfare Policy and Law of the Columbia University School of Social Work has received funds from O.E.O. to enable it to aid neighborhood legal centers, advise attorneys who take welfare cases, and help individuals with legal problems involving welfare agencies. Still another organization is the National Office for the Rights of the Indigent, established in 1967 with the help of a Ford Foundation grant; it maintains a staff of lawyers "who assist in key cases involving the rights of the poor . . . [and] develops strategy for the bringing of test cases likely to make legal precedents that will vindicate the rights of the indigent." [12] Legal activity in the welfare field has grown sufficiently to justify issuance of a bi-monthly survey of pertinent cases, rulings, and decisions—the *Welfare Law Bulletin* published by the Project on Social Welfare Law of New York University Law School.

LANDMARK COURT DECISIONS ON RESIDENCE RULES

Welfare litigation has served to bring up basic issues for judicial review for the first time in the 32-year history of the Public Assistance program. Several recent decisions have far-reaching implications for the future of the direct-aid system.

Residence requirements for eligibility for Public Assistance, which have been applicable in 41 states, now have an uncertain future, dependent on what the Supreme Court

---

[12] Leroy D. Clark, assistant counsel for the National Office for the Rights of the Indigent, testimony, Senate Finance Committee, Sept. 18, 1967.

eventually determines. Cases attacking residence regulations were filed in a half-dozen states in 1967. Federal courts in Connecticut, Delaware and the District of Columbia found the restrictions unconstitutional on the ground that they violated the right of applicants to equal protection of the laws. A federal three-judge panel in Connecticut accepted also the argument that the residence rules abridged a needy person's right to travel freely from state to state.

The District of Columbia case was of particular interest nationally because the capital city is governed by Congress and the case involved a challenge to a one-year residence requirement fixed by act of Congress. A special three-judge court threw out the rule on Nov. 8, 1967, by a 2-1 decision; it held that the delay occasioned by the rule "perpetuates the conditions [of poverty] the legislation is designed to cure."

The ultimate effect of forbidding residence requirements would be to encourage uniformity of benefits from state to state. Officials in communities with relatively generous benefits for public assistance recipients have already expressed concern over an expected influx of poor persons unable to support themselves. In a dissent from the majority opinion in the District of Columbia case, U.S. District Judge Alexander Holtzoff said that if the ban on residence rules was upheld by the Supreme Court, most of the states' relief systems would have to be "revamped, transformed and reorganized."

ATTACK ON 'MAN IN THE HOUSE' DISQUALIFICATION

Another case attracting national attention concerned Alabama's effort to discourage an accretion of illegitimate children on relief rolls. A state rule had required removal of families from A.F.D.C. rolls if the mother was found to be having extramarital relations. The justification for the rule was that the benefit was available only to families of "dependent" children—that is, children without a father or substitute father to provide for them—and that a sexual alliance between the mother and a man not her husband constituted a supposition that the man was a "substitute father." Critics considered the Alabama rule punitive and an attempt to regulate the moral behavior of the poor that would not be tolerated outside the welfare system.

The rule was challenged in a suit brought by a Selma mother of four who had been receiving Public Assistance to supplement her $16 weekly earnings as a waitress. The benefits were cut off when welfare officials accused the woman of having had sexual relations with a married man, even though he was living with his wife and eight children.

A special three-judge federal court at Montgomery held the "substitute father" regulation unconstitutional, and on Nov. 8, 1967, it ordered Alabama to restore to the beneficiary rolls 15,000 to 20,000 children eliminated under the rule. U.S. Supreme Court Justice Hugo L. Black on Nov. 28 stayed the order for 30 days to give the state time to file an appeal.

The Alabama case is of keen interest because it strikes at the heart of a major source of mutual animosity between welfare authorities and welfare recipients. A complaint often raised against A.F.D.C. is that it encourages illegitimacy and parental irresponsibility by providing assurance in advance that the offspring of an illicit union will be supported by the state. There has long been a feeling among some welfare officials that "dependent" (that is, fatherless) children would be supported by their mothers' sexual partners if the state did not step in to relieve them of that responsibility.

The consequence of this thinking is the so-called "substitute father" or "man in the house" rule, perhaps the most despised of all welfare rules among young A.F.D.C. mothers. Some 18 states [13] and the District of Columbia have a "man in the house" rule of some kind. Supreme Court decision in the Alabama case will constitute the first test of the constitutionality of a rule which in effect assumes that responsibility for support of children rests on a man who is not related to them by blood or marriage.

BILL OF COMPLAINTS ABOUT WELFARE PRACTICES

Most of the legal actions taken on behalf of welfare applicants and clients are not momentous in their potential effect on the system as a whole. But the cases give a sampling of the host of long-smoldering grievances the poor have held against the welfare system. In large degree, the complaints are directed not so much against provisions of welfare law as against ways in which the program is carried out in the

---

[13] Arkansas, Arizona, Connecticut, Indiana, Louisiana, Maine, Michigan, Mississippi, Missouri, New Hampshire, New Mexico, North Carolina, Oklahoma, South Carolina, Texas, Tennessee, Vermont, and Virginia.

localities. The numerous humiliations of being on relief, the "snooping" of investigators, the nocturnal searches for a "man in the house," the threats of withdrawal of benefits, the fear of offending the case worker, and, always, the insufficiency of funds to meet the costs of even minimal living expenses—these make up the fabric of discontent which clouds the welfare client's view of the system.

"The enormous power that case workers have over the lives of their clients . . . discourages clients from complaining of abusive practices or availing themselves of the statutory right to a fair hearing," Leroy D. Clark of the National Office for the Rights of the Indigent and the N.A.A.C.P. Legal Defense Fund, said in his testimony before the Senate Finance Committee. A canvass of attorneys in 15 states who had become interested in welfare problems disclosed the following among many grievances:

1. Delays in determining eligibility of applicants, despite provisions of federal law requiring "reasonable promptness" and federal and state regulations prescribing decisions within 30 days.

2. Denial of the right to a hearing on an unfavorable decision, delays in holding hearings, and, especially, enforcement of an administrative decision (such as reduction of a benefit) *before* the hearing to determine its justification has been held.

3. Hearing procedures which fail to conform to regulations on fairness: lack of opportunity to refute testimony and, in one state, the use of a tape recorder rather than a hearing officer to receive testimony.

4. Failure to tell a client why his benefit is reduced or why he is to be cut off relief. "Failure to comply with department policies" and "no longer eligible" are among stock phrases used to inform a client of the decision.

5. Searches and investigations in violation of Fourth Amendment guarantees. California's Supreme Court held in March 1967 that consent of a client to a "midnight raid" by a welfare investigator had no standing because of the threat of being cut off from relief if consent was refused. A new federal regulation, effective July 1, 1967, prescribes safeguards against "practices that violate the individual's privacy or personal dignity," such as entering homes by force or under false pretenses or during "sleeping hours." Nevertheless, abuses of this kind are still reported.

6. Waiting period between a father's desertion and the time when a family can qualify for relief. The minimum waiting period was reported as one month in Kentucky, two months in Alabama and Illinois, three in California, Louisiana, New Hampshire, Ohio and Wisconsin, and six months in Maine, Michigan, Mississippi, Texas and Vermont.

7. The "employable mother" rule in states which withhold A.F.D.C. benefits if the mother declines available work.

The last-mentioned rule is perhaps the most widely condemned of all public welfare rules. Certain states have been charged with manipulating the "employable mother" rule for the purpose of recruiting a force of cheap labor in crop picking season. The N.A.A.C.P. Legal Defense Fund is supporting a suit to enjoin the State of Georgia from terminating A.F.D.C. benefits to mothers at such times.

INADEQUACY OF BENEFITS IN VIEW OF LIVING COSTS

Among all grievances of the poor against the welfare system, none is more basic than the meagerness of the sums provided to meet living costs. This grievance was given support by an Advisory Council on Public Welfare appointed by H.E.W. Secretary John W. Gardner at the direction of Congress to review administration of the public assistance-child welfare programs and recommend improvements in the programs. The council reported in 1966 that "Public assistance payments to needy families and individuals fall seriously below what this nation has proclaimed to be the 'poverty level.'" [14]

Under the law it is the responsibility of the states to determine the level of benefits to be paid persons eligible for Public Assistance. A designated state agency prepares a budget representing what is considered the minimum level of support necessary to maintain a person in health and decency. However, in fewer than one-half of the states does the amount actually paid to A.F.D.C. recipients equal the state's own minimal standard. In this respect, the dependent child program is the least favored; whereas Old Age Assistance payments in January 1967 amounted to 100 per cent of the state standard in 35 states, A.F.D.C. benefits amounted to 100 per cent in only 23 states and was less than 50 per cent in 12 states.

"Many states place arbitrary ceilings on the amount of assistance that can actually be paid, ceilings which may be substantially lower than the minimum need as determined by the state itself." [15] Nor is there any requirement that the standards be re-evaluated periodically. The tendency is for adjustments to lag behind actual increases in the cost of living. Under Secretary of H.E.W. Wilbur J. Cohen told the Senate Finance Committee during hearings in August 1967

[14] Advisory Council on Public Welfare, "*Having the Power, We Have the Duty*" (June 29, 1966), p. 15.
[15] H.E.W. Under Secretary Wilbur J. Cohen, testimony, Senate Finance Committee, Aug. 22, 1967.

that only 25 states had standards which had been brought up to date within the past two years; several states had not revised their standards for 10 years or more.

Welfare mothers have occasionally given public officials vivid insight into the realities of living on Public Assistance. Hearings before the U.S. Civil Rights Commission and its advisory groups in the states have afforded such opportunities to penetrate the wall between the framers of welfare policy and the actual recipients of its benefits. The commission report on its investigation of the A.F.D.C. program in Cleveland, presented as a typical example of how dependent children fare in large cities today, gave a grim picture of poverty and privation: children kept home from school for lack of clothes, wretched housing with flooding toilets, food shortages, unending indebtedness. Even with the aid of food stamps, monthly checks would not stretch more than two or three weeks. An investigator asked: When the money runs low, do you give the children a milk substitute? "Sometimes you can't even afford the substitute," the mother replied.[16]

In another study, the commission found that though the Indiana Public Welfare Department estimated that a mother with three children needed at least $237 a month, the maximum payable under state law was $126. A mother in Gary said: "I have heard people say . . . we have it so easy. . . . Let them come forward, smell the garbage in the summer time, fight the rats, freeze in the winter time. . . . Let him . . . try to feed five children from 17 to 5 on $167 a month." [17]

Future Shape of Dependency Problem

THE MUCH-MALIGNED Public Assistance program began benignly enough in the midst of the worst depression in the nation's history, when poverty was far more prevalent than it is today. As the first permanent system of direct cash assistance to the poor in which the federal government shared the cost, it was hailed at the time of its inception under the Social Security Act of 1935 as a sign of a new era of humaneness in government. Together with other innovat-

[16] U.S. Civil Rights Commission, *Children in Need* (1966), p. 14.
[17] U.S. Commission on Civil Rights, *A Time to Listen . . . A Time to Act* (November 1967), p. 30.

ing programs authorized by the act, it established a national policy of assuring that no person in the country would be allowed to suffer total destitution.

In addition to establishing the Social Security system of retirement benefits and the Unemployment Compensation system, the 1935 act inaugurated a system of federal-state-local cost-sharing of direct aid to three categories of needy persons. The three aid-to-the-needy programs were named: (1) Old Age Assistance, comprising persons over the age of 65; (2) Aid to the Blind; and (3) Aid to Dependent Children in families with no breadwinner. A fourth category—Aid to the Permanently and Totally Disabled—was added in 1950, and in 1962 the Dependent Children program was renamed Aid to Families with Dependent Children to take into account the inclusion of parents or other adult caretakers as beneficiaries.

It was expected in 1935 that, as Social Security insurance programs matured and other measures for economic recovery became operative, the residual relief burden would diminish to the point where responsibility could be returned to state and local governments. Instead, the dependency burden not only grew; it grew in a fashion undreamed of by framers of the original program. Aid to Dependent Children, which began as the smallest of the Public Assistance programs, designed primarily to keep widowed mothers at home with their small children, grew to become by far the largest, and it lost its early widow-and-orphan character. The typical dependent-child family today is fatherless, but not because of death.

Growth of Public Assistance rolls as a whole has accelerated in recent years. By September 1967, 8.6 million persons were receiving support payments—2.9 million more than in 1957. One in every 23 Americans is now on Public Assistance.[18]

Old Age Assistance rolls declined, as expected. The number today is about the same as in 1940—close to two million—but incidence is down by one-half: 109 rather than 217 per 1,000 population over 65. Aid to the Blind has fallen from a peak of 110,000 in the late 1950s to 83,000. Aid to the Totally and Permanently Disabled has moved up steadily

---

[18] The current rate of 40 per 1,000 population compares with 34 in 1957. The rate was 54 at its peak in 1940, and 26 at its lowest in 1945.

from 69,000 in its first year (1950), but it is still a relatively small segment of the total at 629,000 (September 1967).

A General Assistance category, outside the federal cost-sharing system and consisting of local and/or state poor relief, is usually included in tallies of Public Assistance totals. It was by far the largest category in the early years of the federal-aid system; at its peak in 1938, there were nearly twice as many on its rolls (5.3 million) as in all federal-aid categories (3 million). But the number dropped sharply during World War II and has remained relatively low; the trend in the 1960s had been down from over 1 million in 1960-1961, but in recent months it has been climbing to 729,000 in September. The poorest-paying of the direct aid categories, General Assistance has been the only one open to non-disabled males in the working years.[19] The freeze on A.F.D.C. rolls in the 1967 Social Security Amendments could shift a number of needy children to General Assistance.

PREPONDERANCE OF CHILDREN ON PUBLIC ASSISTANCE

The extraordinary growth of Aid to Families with Dependent Children is the source of most of the wrangling over welfare. Beginning with 404,000 in 1936, this program has experienced only two periods of decline, both during war years (1941-1944 and 1950-1953) when jobs were plentiful and poor-family income was boosted by allotments from servicemen's pay. In recent years, however, the number has climbed unchecked by stimulants to the general economy.

More than 5 million persons in 1,244,000 families were receiving A.F.D.C. support in September 1967; 3.84 million of them were children.[20] The proportion of all children under 18 who are on relief has risen from 3 per cent in 1957 to 5.2 per cent (June 1967 estimate), the highest rate in the program's history and twice the 1941 rate. At its lowest ebb, in 1945, only 1½ per cent of all children were on relief. A U.S. welfare official attributed the upward trend to "growth in the child population; an increased number of broken

---

[19] Except for unemployed fathers of dependent children in 22 states, which make such provision under the permissive terms of a 1961 amendment to the Social Security Act.

[20] Extension of benefits to adult caretakers of dependent children in 1950 and later liberalizations of criteria for adult eligibility contributed to over-all growth.

families; the effect of the war on poverty which has focused attention on the vast amount of unmet need . . .; and increasing urbanization, which brings to the cities people ill-equipped with the education and skills required to compete in the urban labor market." [21]

The new assertiveness of the poor in demanding welfare "rights" has apparently affected the growth pattern. Normally the number on A.F.D.C. rolls begins to rise with the approach of winter and begins to fall in the spring. In 1966 the spring dip began, as expected, in May, but the rise began early—in July rather than October. In 1967, the monthly tallies through September showed no seasonal dip at all, but a continuing climb each spring and summer month.

UNEVENNESS OF WELFARE BURDEN; PLIGHT OF CITIES

Public Assistance in all forms cost the taxpayer $6.8 billion in fiscal 1967—twice what it did a decade earlier and nearly one-fourth more than in 1966. The payments constituted nine-tenths of one per cent of Gross National Product: that percentage has moved up slowly since 1955 when it was a little under seven-tenths of one per cent.

All of the increase is not due to added enrollment; added services have been costly too. Payment for medical care has became an increasingly significant cost factor; in September 1967, for example, that item alone amounted to $245,205,000 or well over one-half the amount paid to all recipients for basic living expenses ($423,307,000). Between July 1966 and July 1967 payment for medical services rose more than 40 per cent while direct money payments to recipients rose 14 per cent.

Financing problems are exacerbated by the unevenness of the welfare burden on different states and on different localities within each state. The proportion of the population receiving assistance, as of December 1966, ranged from 8 per cent in Mississippi to 1.4 per cent in Indiana. Among the 12 states with rates higher than the national average (3.8 per cent) were some of the richest and some of the poorest.[22]

States vary greatly in outlays for welfare, depending on

---

[21] John J. Hurley, acting director, Bureau of Family Services, Welfare Administration, U.S. Department of Health, Education, and Welfare, testimony, House Appropriations Subcommittee, April 14, 1967.

[22] Alabama, Arkansas, California, Colorado, Kentucky, Louisiana, Mississippi, Missouri, New Mexico, New York, Oklahoma, West Virginia.

size and on the character of the needy population, their ability to pay, and the prevailing attitude of authorities toward the poor. Welfare policy is still colored by fear that a truly adequate benefit schedule would encourage sloth and parasitism. Oklahoma makes the largest outlay relative to personal income ($9.44 per $1,000), while Virginia makes the smallest ($1.03 per $1,000). In terms of amount spent per inhabitant, California ranks first with nearly $30, while Virginia is again lowest, spending $2.45 per capita.[23]

The fiscal crisis in welfare is centered largely in the cities to which the poor and otherwise disadvantaged have migrated in great numbers. The "welfare boom," Mayor Lindsay told the Senate Finance Committee, Sept. 20, 1967, had "victimized" his city: New York's relief rolls were growing at the rate of 12,000 or more a month; by late November the total caseload was close to 800,000.

The fiscal plight of the cities and the immensity of the welfare problem have encouraged a trend toward more state responsibility for poor relief. Twenty-eight states now have state administration of local welfare. The Massachusetts legislature has authorized transfer to state operation on July 1, 1968. New York voters turned down in November a proposed new state constitution that would have required a state takeover by 1970, but the issue there is by no means dead. Gov. Nelson A. Rockefeller said on Nov. 17 that he favored assumption of local welfare costs by the state.

SEARCH FOR SUBSTITUTES FOR THE EXISTING SYSTEM

Solutions to the problems presented by the growth of dependency are elusive. Many proposals have been put forth and reforms adopted, but nearly all tend to create new difficulties. It is universally agreed that it would be better if the poor could earn their own way and not depend on government handouts. But efforts to convert relief recipients into wage-earners present many obstacles. Aside from emotion-charged controversies over coercion and the effects on small children of having their mothers go out to work, there is the question of cost. It is much more expensive to provide training and job-placement services for unskilled and poorly educated welfare recipients than to give them direct aid, especially if day care or foster home facilities must be provided for workers' children. In addition, organized labor is wary

---

[23] These figures represent expenditures for Public Assistance from state and local sources only in the year ended June 30, 1966.

of work projects for the poor that would cause an influx of wage-cutting competition in the labor market. Among the poor themselves there is fear of being forced into low-paying, menial work.

Support is growing for some form of minimum income guarantee to provide a blanket payment to all persons or families below an established poverty level.[24] The chief advantages of such a plan are that it would fill the gaps in coverage which exist under the present system, eliminate much of the present cost of administering direct aid to the poor, remove the necessity for "snooping" which is a major source of irritation in client-welfare relations, and free welfare agencies to concentrate on helping families overcome problems that cause dependency.

The President of the Ford Motor Co., Arjay Miller, is the first big-business executive to come out publicly for a form of universally guaranteed income. In a speech before the National Industrial Conference Board in New York, Nov. 30, 1967, Miller said he favored a negative income tax, a plan by which federal funds would be paid automatically, in the manner of tax refunds, to individuals filing forms showing below-standard income. "It is from poverty that many other social ills spring," Miller said, "and any successful effort to eliminate or greatly reduce this malignant growth could bring about dramatic improvement in the general health of our society." The U. S. Office of Economic Opportunity approved a grant last year to the University of Wisconsin Institute for Research on Poverty to conduct a pilot project to demonstrate whether some form of guaranteed income would be a preferred substitute for the present system.

The extent to which the guaranteed income concept has taken hold among social planners is indicated in the tentative planning of applicants to the Department of Housing and Urban Development for model-city demonstration grants. At least 15 of the 63 cities which received planning grants are considering the incorporation of some form of guaranteed income experimentation in their overall projects. Among these cities are Boston, Detroit, East St. Louis, Newark, Oakland, and Trenton.

---

[24] See "Guaranteed Income Plan," *E.R.R.*, 1966 Vol. I, p. 399.

BLACK PRIDE

by

Richard L. Worsnop

1 9 6 8
Sept. 11

BLACK PRIDE

THE NEGRO REVOLUTION in the United States has acquired a new mood and direction under a new generation of leaders. The old goal of integration—assimilation of Negroes into white American society—is now widely rejected, at least for the time being, as a form of "painless genocide." The new goals include racial pride, cultural separateness, and economic and political self-sufficiency. The word "Negro" itself is falling into disfavor; "black" or "Afro-American" are often preferred, especially among younger people.

Until around three years ago, the Negro civil rights movement was basically a middle-class movement. The South was the principal battleground. Federal legislation barring racial discrimination in such fields as voting, public accommodations, education, and housing was the major objective. Active participation of white people in the movement was welcomed. The newly emerging Negro leaders, in contrast, seem concerned primarily with problems of the lower-class black ghettos of big cities outside the South. Civil rights laws are generally dismissed as irrelevant to the needs of ghetto blacks. White financial support of the movement is still accepted, but whites are less welcome than formerly in decision-making positions.

EMERGENCE OF THE CONCEPT OF BLACK POWER

The slogan of the Negro revolution today is "black power" —an ill-defined concept that many whites find menacing. LeRoi Jones, the writer, describes it thus: "Black Power, the power to control our lives ourselves. All of our lives. Our laws. Our culture. Our children. Their lives. Our total consciousness, black oriented. . . . Black power must be spiritually, emotionally, and historically in tune with black people, as well as serving their economic and political ends." [1] Newspaper columnist Charles Bartlett observed last July 11

---

[1] LeRoi Jones, "The Need for a Cultural Base to Civil Rites & Bpower Mooments," *The Black Power Revolt* (1968), Floyd B. Barbour, ed., pp. 119, 121.

that, "stripped of hostile overtones, the concept of black power is simply . . . that black Americans must create for themselves an environment which is conducive to their psychological health and institutional strength." He added: "They must narrow the gap between their own sense of inferiority and the white man's sense of superiority before they can hope to live as equals."

Bartlett's definition evidently is shared by two of the older Negro civil rights organizations, the National Association for the Advancement of Colored People and the National Urban League. Addressing the Congress of Racial Equality's annual convention in Columbus, Ohio, July 5, 1968, Roy Wilkins, executive director of N.A.A.C.P., asserted that cooperative efforts among Negroes were "a necessity if black people are going to successfully attack the problems that beset them." But Wilkins cautioned: "In teaching race pride it will be disastrous if we teach a false distinction and a false superiority. . . . Pride, yes. The will to achieve, yes. Equal acceptance with other members of the human family, yes. But arrogance, bombast, and contrived myths, no."

Whitney M. Young Jr., Urban League Director, told the CORE convention the following day that his organization supported "as legitimate and historically consistent a minority's mobilization of its economic and political power to reward its friends and punish its enemies." Young went on to say that Negroes were "no longer enchanted with being near white people" and that they had found white institutions were "not all they were put up to be." He urged Negroes to use their own organizations to build "the power that America respects."

INSISTENCE ON UNIQUE NEGRO CULTURAL IDENTITY

Establishment of a distinct black cultural identity within white society is a key element in the movement to enhance the power of black people generally. A study made public by the National Advisory Commission on Civil Disorders, July 28, 1968, found that "As in the case of religious and ethnic groups in America, there seems to be wide support [among Negroes] for cultural individuality within a larger interracial social structure." For example, the study reported that 42 per cent of all Negroes interviewed in a special opinion survey believed that Negro school children should study an African language; 96 per cent thought that Negroes should take more pride in Negro history.

Black Pride

Black cultural assertiveness can be seen in the growing popularity of African garments and of "Afro" or "natural" (as opposed to "processed" or artificially straightened) hair styles among young Negro men and women. Negroes in New York City have demanded, often successfully, that certain schools, parks and monuments be named or renamed for noted Negroes. A public housing project in Harlem and a music grove in Brooklyn's Prospect Park recently were rechristened in honor of the late Rev. Dr. Martin Luther King Jr.; five new schools in the city are to bear the names of Negroes. In East Palo Alto, Calif., whose population of 27,000 is nearly 70 per cent Negro, a campaign is under way to change the town's name to Nairobi.[2] A legend sometimes seen on posters states that "Black is beautiful and it's so beautiful to be black."

The essence of black cultural identity is said to be "soul" —a word that seems as difficult to define as the German *Gemütlichkeit*. Lerone Bennett, an editor of *Ebony*, has described the term as "the American counterpart of the African concept of Negritude, a distinct quality of Negroness growing out of the Negro's experience and not his genes." [3] A white professor of sociology found through a survey that the word had a great variety of meanings.

> Soul can be many things—a type of food (good food is "soul food," a "bowl of soul"),[4] music, a quality of mind, a total way of acting (in eating, drinking, dancing, walking, talking, relating to others, etc.). The person who acts with soul acts directly and honestly from his heart. He feels it and tells it "like it is." One respondent identified soul with ambition and drive. . . . Another said soul was getting down to the nitty-gritty, that is, moving directly to what is basic without guise and disguise. Thus soul is the opposite of hypocrisy, deceit and phoniness. . . .
>
> Most definitions tied soul directly to Negro experience. As one hustler put it, "It is the ability to survive. We've made it with so much less. Soul is the Negro who has the spirit to sing in slavery to overcome the monotony." With very few exceptions, the men interviewed argued that soul was what Negroes had and whites did not. Negroes were "soul brothers," warm and emotional—whites cold as ice. Like other oppressed minorities, these street Negroes believed they had nothing except their soul and their humanity, and that this made them better than their oppressors.[5]

Ulf Hannerz, of the University of Stockholm's Institute

---

[2] Other suggested names include Dar es Salaam, Kenyatta, Tanganyika, Tanzania, and Uhuru.

[3] Quoted by Ulf Hannerz, "What Negroes Mean by 'Soul,'" *Trans-Action*, July/August 1968, p. 59.

[4] Chitlins, hog maw, black-eyed peas, collard greens, corn bread, grits, etc.

[5] John Horton, "Time and Cool People," *Trans-Action*, April 1967, p. 11.

of Ethnography,[6] believes that the cult of soul reflects the ghetto Negro's "increasingly ambivalent conceptions about the opportunity structure." In the past, according to Hannerz, the disadvantaged Negro could blame his condition on rigid social barriers. But many of the old barriers have since fallen; hence "the suspicion arises that under-achievement is due to one's own failure." It follows that "The motive of the soul vocabulary . . . is above all to reduce self-doubt by persuading soul brothers that they are successful." [7]

PROPOSALS TO MAKE BLACK AREAS SELF-SUFFICIENT

Black control of black ghettos has replaced integration as the immediate goal of most Negro leaders. Some Negroes have gone so far as to demand establishment of a separate black nation within the United States. Prof. Robert S. Browne of Fairleigh Dickinson University contends that such a "homeland" would enable the black community to reclaim a group individuality and to "build its own majority culture." [8] The more widely held aim is black ownership of ghetto shops and businesses and black direction of ghetto schools and police precincts.

The Urban League on July 29, 1968, announced a "New Thrust" program whose objective is to build "ghetto power." Headed by Sterling Tucker, executive director of the Washington (D. C.) Urban League, "New Thrust" is to receive $2 million in "feeder money" from the Urban League in its first year of operation; additional funds are expected from foundations and local community chests. Tucker hopes to set up between 50 and 75 neighborhood "outposts" in city slum areas within a year. These centers will serve as focal points for organizing ghetto residents to press for political and economic power "through all legal means."

The idea of black self-sufficiency has won a certain amount of support among white politicians. Republican presidential nominee Richard M. Nixon asserted in a nation-wide radio address, April 25, 1968, that the way to approach the problems of the ghetto was to provide "incentives to private industry to make acceptable the added risks of ghetto development and of training the unemployed for jobs." Nixon touched on ghetto problems also in his accept-

---

[6] Hannerz has done field work among Washington, D. C., Negroes for two years under a Carnegie Corporaiton grant to the Center for Applied Linguistics for urban-language study.

[7] Ulf Hannerz, *op. cit.*, p. 61.

[8] Remarks before meeting of National Community Advisory Council, San Francisco, July 2, 1968.

ance speech at the Republican National Convention on Aug. 8:

Black Americans—no more than white Americans—do not want more government programs which perpetuate dependency. They don't want to become a colony in a nation. They want the pride and the self-respect and the dignity that can only come if they have an equal chance to own their own homes, to own their own businesses, to be managers and executives as well as workers, to have a piece of the action in the exciting ventures of private enterprise.

Nixon was not the first white politician to advocate such a course. The late Sen. Robert F. Kennedy (D N.Y.) was the author of a bill to provide incentives for both home ownership and new business enterprises in the slums; Sen. Charles Percy (R Ill.) introduced a similar bill with respect to home ownership. Sen. Jacob K. Javits (R N.Y.) has urged creation of a Domestic Development Bank to do for ghetto businessmen what the International Bank for Reconstruction and Development does for developing nations.

The developing-nation analogy is apposite. Because of past discrimination in hiring and promotion, would-be Negro businessmen usually lack the requisite managerial skills. Capital, always in short supply in the ghetto,[9] has become scarcer than ever due to investors' reluctance to put money into riot-prone areas. Moreover, like most developing countries, the ghetto suffers from a "brain drain." White industry now actively recruits bright Negro college graduates; ghetto businesses, almost always small and marginally profitable, are rarely able to offer the graduates comparable opportunities.

While proposals to build up black economic power have stirred little controversy, the demand for black control of ghetto police forces has met strong opposition. Recent disorders in Cleveland furnish a case in point. On the night of July 24, one day after three policemen had been killed from ambush by snipers, Mayor Carl Stokes withdrew all white police and National Guardsmen from the troubled area. Around 500 volunteers from Negro organizations, led by a relatively few Negro policemen, were given the job of keeping the peace. The experiment was successful to the extent that no deaths or shooting incidents took place that night. However, perhaps because 36 businesses were looted and three fires set, Mayor Stokes, a Negro, was sharply criti-

---

[9] Of more than 14,000 commercial banks in the United States, fewer than 20 are operated by Negroes.

cized for his decision. Many rank-and-file policemen and white Clevelanders felt that he had knuckled under to black militants and insulted the police force. The police and National Guard were ordered back into the area of the disturbance on July 25, but criticism of the Mayor continued.[10]

REJECTION OF WHITE ROLE IN BLACK ORGANIZATIONS

Demands for ghetto autonomy have been accompanied by proposals that white persons be excluded from positions of importance in Negro organizations. A position paper drawn up by the Student Non-Violent Coordinating Committee two and one-half years ago asserted that "Negroes in this country have never been allowed to organize themselves because of white interference." It added:

> Blacks, in fact, feel intimidated by the presence of whites, because of their knowledge of the power that whites have over their lives. . . . A climate has to be created whereby blacks can express themselves. The reason that whites must be excluded is not that one is anti-white, but because the efforts that one is trying to achieve cannot succeed because whites have an intimidating effect. . . . This is not to say that whites have not had an important role in the movement. In the case of [the 1964] Mississippi [voter registration drive], their role was very key in that they helped give blacks the right to organize, but that role is now over.
>
> If we were to proceed toward true liberation, we must cut ourselves off from white people. We must form our own institutions, credit unions, co-ops, political parties, write our own histories.[11]

The foregoing sentiments are held not only by S.N.C.C. but also by CORE and militant local Negro organizations such as US, a Los Angeles black power group headed by Ron Karenga, who is affiliated also with the California Black Panthers.[12] Many white liberals who have been active in the Negro civil rights movement inevitably have been offended by efforts to exclude them from further participation in efforts to advance Negro interests. One such person is Saul D. Alinsky, a sociologist who has devoted a large part of his career to organizing the poor.

In a recent letter to the Rev. Lucius Walker, director of

---

[10] Washington, D. C., Public Safety Director Patrick V. Murphy rejected, Sept. 3, proposals that citizens be given a role in internal discipline of the city's police department. Murphy said that, on the contrary, the chief of police "should be given greater authority to discipline the department" and that "if he doesn't do the job well, he should be relieved." Agitation for citizen participation in police affairs in the District of Columbia has come almost exclusively from Negro sections.

[11] See "Negro Power Struggle," *E.R.R.*, 1968 Vol. I, pp. 136-140. The N.A.A.C.P. and the Urban League both have white presidents—in each case a figurehead post.

[12] Karenga served as so-called theoretician of the third National Conference on Black Power, held at Philadelphia from Aug. 29 to Sept. 1, 1968. He was given the job of arranging for a national constitutional convention to organize a national black party through which blacks would take over control of Negro ghettos.

the Interreligious Foundation for Community Organization, Alinsky sharply attacked several black power leaders and their doctrines. Alinsky had applied to IFCO for a $225,000 grant to his Industrial Areas Foundation. But he withdrew the application after reading the transcript of a speech by Karenga, a board member of IFCO, at Dayton, Ohio, on June 22, 1968. Karenga, according to Alinsky, said that IFCO had received an application "from a white organizer who wants to set up a training institute which will surely fail." Karenga reportedly went on to say that "Blacks are a country and if you support America then you are against my community."

Commenting on Karenga's speech in the letter to Walker, Alinsky said that "If a condition of eligibility for a grant from IFCO means not supporting America, then, of course, we are utterly disinterested in receiving a grant and regret having submitted an application." Walker commented: "Black people are just as American as Alinsky. And whatever changes they bring about will reconstitute the American value system." [13]

Decline of the Negro Rights Movement

THE CHANGED NATURE of the Negro civil rights movement is vividly illustrated by the contrast between the August 1963 March on Washington for Jobs and Freedom and the Solidarity Day demonstration in the capital on June 19, 1968.[14] The 1963 march had more than 200,000 participants, many of whom were middle-class whites. An atmosphere of buoyancy and purposefulness prevailed, as epitomized by Dr. King's concluding "I Have a Dream" address. Discipline was strict: All placards carried by marchers were approved in advance by the committee in charge of the demonstration; no acts of civil disobedience were allowed; and portions of a speech by John Lewis, then chairman of the Student Non-Violent Coordinating Committee, were deleted by march leaders as inflammatory and out of keeping with the mood of the day.

Solidarity Day, in contrast, was a somber occasion in-

13 Quoted, *Los Angeles Times*, July 7, 1968.
14 See "Mass Demonstrations," *E.R.R.*, 1963 Vol. II, pp. 585-588.

tended as the climax of the six-week-old Poor People's
Campaign in Washington. The crowd of 50,000 was predominantly black and poor. Speakers expressed anger and
sorrow over the recent assassinations of Dr. King and Sen.
Kennedy, condemned the war in Viet Nam as racist and im-
moral, and warned that Solidarity Day might be the last
peaceful demonstration of its kind. Moreover, the June 19
demonstration had been preceded and was followed by repeated acts of civil disobedience at the Agriculture Department, Justice Department, Supreme Court, and on the
Capitol grounds. The evacuation on June 24 of Resurrection
City, the Poor People's Campaign shantytown near the Lincoln Memorial, precipitated an outbreak of violence in a
predominantly Negro section of Washington.

ATTAINMENT OF THE LEGISLATIVE GOALS OF NEGROES

The five years separating the two mass demonstrations in
Washington brought enactment of federal legislation that
met most of the goals of the 1963 marchers. The Civil Rights
Act of 1964, considerably broader than the bill proposed by
President Kennedy in June 1963, barred racial discrimination (1) in public accommodations; (2) in employment
practices of most businesses; [15] and (3) in any program or
activity receiving federal assistance.

Title I of the Civil Rights Act of 1964 strengthened existing laws against denial of voting rights by prohibiting unequal application of such registration requirements as
literacy tests. The Voting Rights Act of 1965 went further:
It suspended literacy tests and gave the Attorney General
power to appoint federal examiners to supervise voter registration in states or political subdivisions where (1) a test
or similar qualifying device was in force on Nov. 1, 1964,
and (2) fewer than 50 per cent of all voting-age residents
were registered to vote on that date or did actually vote in
the 1964 presidential election.

No major new civil rights legislation was enacted in 1966
or 1967. The House passed an open-housing bill Aug. 16,
1967, but it languished in the Senate. Anger caused by rioting in the black ghettos of numerous cities made Congress
unresponsive to President Johnson's repeated requests for
action on open housing. On March 11, 1968, however, the
Senate, to everyone's surprise, proceeded to pass a far-

---

[15] Job discrimination was defined as discrimination based on race, color, sex, or
national origin.

reaching open-housing bill, and on April 10—six days after the assassination of Dr. King—the House, accepting the Senate version instead of going to conference, speeded the measure to the White House. The President approved it the next day.

The latest civil rights act prohibits discrimination based on race, religion or national origin in the sale or rental of housing. When fully effective on Jan. 1, 1970, the law will cover approximately 80 per cent of all housing in the country. The act also carries federal criminal penalties to be imposed on any person convicted of injuring, intimidating, or interfering with any other person engaged in a number of activities, including voting or campaigning as a candidate in any public election, serving on a federal jury, working for a federal agency, or participating in a federally assisted program or activity. The third major section of the law prescribes penalties for persons convicted of traveling in interstate commerce or using the facilities of interstate commerce with intent to incite, organize, or take part in a riot or assist others to do so.

The effect on Negroes of the federal civil rights legislation, and of similar state legislation enacted in recent years, has been the opposite of what was expected. Instead of finding satisfaction in hard-won victories, the black community as a whole appears to have become more frustrated and angry than ever. Winning the right, say, to sit at a previously all-white lunch counter has produced not gratitude but rage that it took so long to gain recognition of such an elementary right. Above all, it is asserted that open-housing and public-accommodations laws mean little to most ghetto Negroes, because they are too poor to patronize hotels and restaurants or buy a house in the suburbs. Black equality will not be achieved, it is said, until poverty is eliminated.

The trouble is that there is wide disagreement on how to abolish poverty. White sympathizers of the Poor People's Campaign in Washington complained that its leaders never defined their demands clearly. When Bayard Rustin announced a list of "immediate demands" [16] on Congress last June 3, he was promptly dismissed as coordinator of Soli-

16 (1) Creation of a million federally financed "socially useful jobs in public service"; (2) construction of six million new dwellings in the next 10 years; (3) repeal of the "punitive welfare restrictions" in the 1967 amendments to the Social Security Act; (4) extension to farm workers of rights guaranteed in the National Labor Relations Act to organize unions and bargain collectively; (5) restoration of congressional budget cuts for bilingual education, Head Start, summer jobs, the Economic Opportunity Act, and the Elementary and Secondary Education Act.

darity Day for being "out of order." Sterling Tucker, Rustin's replacement as coordinator, issued a revised and less precise set of demands on June 9. Tucker called for an end to poverty and violence in American life, a "national commitment to provide a meaningful job at a living wage for every employable citizen," a governmental guarantee of a "secure and adequate income for all who cannot find jobs" or cannot work because of infirmity, and an "end to hunger and malnutrition in America."

PERSISTING DISCRIMINATION IN EVERYDAY NEGRO LIFE

A significant development in the Negro struggle for equality is the increasing involvement of middle-class Negroes in ghetto problems. The Negro middle class has been sharply criticized in the past for its aloofness from such problems and for its eagerness to adopt the mores and trappings of white society. The late E. Franklin Frazier wrote that "When the opportunity has been present, the black bourgeoisie has exploited the Negro masses as ruthlessly as have whites."

> As the intellectual leaders in the Negro community, they have never dared think beyond a narrow, opportunistic philosophy that provided a rationalization for their own advantages. Although the black bourgeoisie exercise considerable influence on the values of Negroes, they do not occupy a dignified position in the Negro community. The masses regard the black bourgeoisie as simply those who have been "lucky in getting money" which enables them to engage in conspicuous consumption. When this class pretends to represent the best manners or morals of the Negro, the masses regard such claims as hypocrisy.[17]

Today, much of the black middle class has come to accept the ghetto view that Negroes should think and develop as black people and not accept white models of behavior and aspiration. "When they start talking about Negroes, I say I'm a Negro too," Leon Coward, director of a day care center in New York City, has said. "But my brother down there [in the ghetto], he could kick me in my pants, 'cause he knows I've got a bellyful, and his is empty. Now we're getting to the point where I am beginning to recognize this man's empty belly."[18]

The changing attitude of more affluent Negroes stems partly from realization that material success seldom is

[17] E. Franklin Frazier, *Black Bourgeoisie* (1962 Collier Books edition), p. 194.
[18] Quoted by Roger Beardwood, "The New Negro Mood," *Fortune*, January 1968, p. 151.

Black Pride

accompanied by social acceptance and professional equality. This is so even in the world of professional sports, according to a recent series of articles by Jack Olsen in *Sports Illustrated*. The burden of Olsen's series was that Negro professional athletes, commonly thought to be competing on equal terms against whites, are discriminated against in many ways. "Black professional athletes say they are underpaid, shunted into certain stereotyped positions and treated like sub-humans by Paleolithic coaches who regard them as watermelon-eating idiots."

> In baseball the Negro usually will find himself in the outfield, less often playing the infield and least often performing as a member of the battery. Only 13 of the 207 pitchers on major league rosters this summer are Negroes. In the pro football leagues, . . . the Negro is never permitted to be a quarterback, and one can only pity the black athlete who played the position in college. . . . Aside from matters of man-to-man prejudice, the black professional athlete makes two major complaints: that he must be significantly better than his white counterpart, and that when he is through as a competitor his sport has no use for him.[19]

Bill Russell of the Boston Celtics is the only Negro manager of a major professional sports team, and Jim Gilliam of the Los Angeles Dodgers is the only Negro coach among the 20 major-league teams. Monte Irvin, a former player for the New York Giants, became the first Negro appointed to a high administrative post in baseball when he started work Sept. 2, 1968, as an assistant to Commissioner William D. Eckert.

Black athletes formerly kept their complaints about discriminatory treatment to themselves, but no longer. Moreover, they are under increasing pressure to use their prestige to make themselves a force in the improvement of the Negro community. Harry Edwards, a former athletic star and now a sociology instructor at San Jose (Calif.) State College, has asserted that "As long as you have black athletes making it to the top and then shutting up like Uncle Willie Mays, or like Jesse Owens or Joe Louis, well, athletics has done very little for the black community."

> It has helped black individuals to delude themselves, this is all. But when you have people speaking out like Jackie Robinson, Bill Russell and Oscar Robertson, you begin to feel the importance of sports to the black community. When you have people like Satch Sanders going out and getting a million-dollar grant from the federal government to revitalize housing in the black community of

---

[19] Jack Olsen, "The Black Athlete—Part 4," *Sports Illustrated*, July 22, 1968, pp. 29, 34.

Boston—well, they don't give it to him because he was some Joe off the street, but because he was Satch Sanders of the Celtics and because he had made himself a public figure and had access to the white man's media and public opinion forces.

In short, "Nowadays the Negro community will respect the black competitor, but the respect will not last if the athlete confines his activities to the field." [20]

THREAT OF NEGRO ATHLETES TO BOYCOTT OLYMPICS

Black college athletes are no less militant than their counterparts in professional sports. Under the leadership of Harry Edwards, numerous black track and field stars boycotted an indoor meet sponsored by the New York Athletic Club in February 1968. Edwards also is the leader of the Olympic Project for Human Rights, a loosely organized group of black college athletes who intend to stage some sort of protest at the Olympic Games in Mexico City in October.

Edwards' original aim apparently was to organize a black boycott of the various trials in which the American team is selected. Such a boycott would have drastically lowered this country's chances of winning gold medals in basketball and in short-distance track events, among other areas of competition. A number of Negro college basketball stars, including Lew Alcindor of U.C.L.A., did decline to enter the Olympic trials. But Edwards announced on Aug. 31 that black athletes would not boycott the Olympics because only about one-half of them were willing to do so. Instead, Edwards said, they would wear black armbands and refuse to participate in awards ceremonies and victory marches.

Image of Negro in Arts and Education

A PRIME COMPLAINT of Negroes is that they are ignored in American history textbooks and caricatured in the entertainment media. As a result, it is charged, both white prejudices and black feelings of inferiority are reinforced. But remedial steps are being taken in both fields. High school texts emphasizing contributions to the country made by American Negroes are being rushed into print. Several col-

[20] Quoted by Jack Olsen, "The Black Athlete—Part I," *Sports Illustrated*, July 1, 1968, p. 18.

leges have introduced or are planning to introduce courses in Negro culture. And the National Broadcasting Company on Sept. 17 will introduce *Julia,* the first family-type situation comedy series with a Negro star to be shown regularly on television.[21]

ATTACK ON NEGRO STEREOTYPES IN ENTERTAINMENT

Hollywood has been criticized for presenting a false image of Negroes on film ever since the release of *Birth of a Nation* in 1915. In some silent films, Negro parts were played by white actors in blackface. When Negro character players such as Hattie McDaniel, Louise Beavers, Mantan Moreland and Stepin Fetchit began to appear in films in the 1930s, they were confined almost exclusively to comedy or servant roles. In general, Negroes were portrayed in films of that era as lazy, bulgy-eyed buffoons.[22] Lena Horne, who appeared in several movie musicals in the 1940s, recalls that the scenes in which she sang were shot separately so that they could be scissored out when the films were shown in the South.

Negroes moved into starring film roles around 15 years ago with the arrival in Hollywood of such performers as Harry Belafonte, Sidney Poitier, Sammy Davis, and the late Dorothy Dandridge. There followed a burst of all-Negro "specials"—*Carmen Jones, Porgy and Bess, Anna Lucasta, St. Louis Woman.* But fault was found with these also. James Baldwin asserted that *"Carmen Jones* does not inhabit the never-never land of such bogus but rather entertaining works as *Stormy Weather* or *Cabin in the Sky* [23]— in which at least one could listen to the music; *Carmen Jones* has moved into a stratosphere rather more interesting and pernicious, in which even Negro speech is parodied out of its charm and liberalized, if one may so put it, out of its force and precision."

The result is not that the characters sound like everybody else, which would be bad enough; the result is that they sound ludicrously false and affected, like ante-bellum Negroes imitating their masters. This is also the way they look, and also the way they are dressed,

---

[21] One of the recommendations of the National Advisory Commission on Civil Disorders was that "Negroes should appear more frequently in dramatic and comedy series" on television.

[22] However, Stepin Fetchit took exception to a July 2, 1968, Columbia Broadcasting System television show—"Black History—Lost, Stolen or Strayed"—which used film clips from his movies to show the old Hollywood stereotype of the Negro. "It was 'Step' who elevated the Negro to the dignity of a Hollywood star," he said on July 24. "If it wasn't for me, there wouldn't have been any Martin Luther King or any of these others."

[23] Two earlier film musicals with all-Negro casts.

and the word that springs immediately to mind to describe the appallingly technicolored sets . . . is "spotless." They could easily have been dreamed up by someone determined to prove that Negroes are as "clean" and "modern" as white people and, I suspect, in one way or another, that is exactly how they *were* dreamed up.[24]

The main complaint about treatment of Negroes on television has been that few Negroes, until recently, were given continuing roles in dramatic or comedy series. For example, a television monitoring survey taken in 1964 by the Committee on Integration of the New York Society for Ethical Culture reported that, in a five-hour viewing period, only three Negroes were likely to be seen on the TV screen, and that two of them would appear for less than a minute. Negroes were most likely to be seen, the report stated, on news and informational programs.[25]

COMPLAINTS ABOUT CREATION OF A NEW STEREOTYPE

Negroes are featured more prominently today than formerly on television programs. But it is asserted that these programs have created a new Negro stereotype—the black "second banana." The pattern was set in the 1965 season, when Robert Culp and Bill Cosby, the Negro comedian, co-starred in the highly successful adventure series *I Spy.* Since then, several other dramatic series with Negro supporting players have been introduced—*Mission: Impossible* with Greg Morris; *Ironside,* with Don Mitchell; *N.Y.P.D.,* with Robert Hooks, among others. In each case, the Negro actor plays a clearly secondary role with respect to a white star or stars, and he rarely is involved in a romantic situation.

Diahann Carroll, who will become the first Negro to star in a regular television series, *Julia,* will play the part of a young widow with a five-year-old son; they live, according to Robert Lewis Shayon of *Saturday Review,* in "a plush, middle-class, suburban apartment" and have kindly white neighbors. "Though this situation might exist in the few interracial neighborhoods which have evolved," Shayon writes, "it is all a far, far cry from the bitter realities of Negro life in the urban ghetto, the pit of America's explosion potential."

In the fantasy of *Julia,* Corey's father is nobly dead in Viet Nam; in the reality of the ghettos, the Negro adults have, in major pro-

---

[24] James Baldwin, "Carmen Jones: The Dark Is Light Enough," *Notes of a Native Son* (1957 Beacon paperback edition), pp. 48-49.
[25] "The Negro in Television," *The Negro Handbook* (1966), p. 362.

portions, simply disappeared—unable to get work, to support wives and children, to maintain their own and their families' respect. What curious irony that this well-meaning TV program should contribute to the castration theme in the history of the American Negro male. The Negro female accommodates to the white power structure; the Negro male is aggressive in his demands for responsibility, and such aggression would hardly be welcome in a TV series.[26]

Similar criticism has been directed at the recent films of Sidney Poitier, who was ranked fifth among the top male movie stars in terms of box-office appeal in a recent poll by *Boxoffice* magazine. Poitier became the first Negro recipient of an Academy of Motion Picture Arts and Sciences best-acting award when he won an Oscar for his role in the 1963 picture *Lilies of the Field.*[27] In that film, Poitier played a drifter who helped a group of nuns build a church. His subsequent films included *A Patch of Blue,* in which he befriended a blind white girl, and *Guess Who's Coming to Dinner?* in which he was engaged to be married to a white girl.

These and other Poitier roles have given rise to charges that the actor is creating a "Noble Negro" stereotype. Foster Hirsch wrote late last year in a small New York literary magazine, *Readers & Writers,* that Poitier's films "have substituted a myth in place of a direct and honest confrontation with the position of the Negro in American society." Hirsch asserted that "The characters Poitier plays are too unrealistic and limited to continue to have force, and his screen image is fast becoming as much a stereotype as the servants and mammies of earlier days." [28]

Poitier agrees with some of the criticism directed at him. But he retorts that, as the only black star now working regularly in American films, he has little choice except to play the kind of roles he has been offered. Poitier has formed his own film production company, E&R Productions. From this company, *Ebony* predicts, "will surely come the kind of films [Poitier] says he has always wanted to make—films whose comments are not trapped in the narrow confines of racism." [29]

Up Tight!, a film now in production, promises to be the

---

[26] Robert Lewis Shayon, "'Julia': Breakthrough or Letdown?" *Saturday Review,* April 20, 1968, p. 49.

[27] Hattie McDaniel won a best-supporting-actress Oscar in 1939 for *Gone With the Wind.*

[28] Quoted by Charles L. Sanders, "Sidney Poitier: The Man Behind the Superstar," *Ebony,* April 1968, p. 174.

[29] *Ibid.,* pp. 179-180.

most controversial movie to date about Negroes. Based loosely on *The Informer*, a 1935 film about the secret Irish Republican Brotherhood, *Up Tight!* shows the activities of black militants in the Hough area of Cleveland. Similarly, a new television series called *The Outcasts* will treat black-white relations in blunter than usual terms. The co-stars of the series portray a former slave and a former slave owner teamed as bounty hunters in the post-Civil War West. According to Jackie Cooper, vice president of Screen Gems, the two main characters in *The Outcasts* will rarely be cordial to each other.

CRITICISM OF TREATMENT OF NEGROES IN TEXTBOOKS

The campaign to combat neglect in public schools of Negro contributions to American history is making rapid progress in many communities. Eighth-graders attending summer classes at the Wanamaker Middle School in Philadelphia this year were given a special course on black power. Public schools in Montgomery County, Maryland, a predominantly white county adjacent to Washington, D. C., are beginning this autumn to teach the history and literature of the American Negro. A high school in New York City has introduced, at the request of Negro students, a course in the Swahili language.

Negroes seem increasingly distrustful of white accounts of slavery in the United States. The reaction of black writers to William Styron's 1967 novel *The Confessions of Nat Turner* provides a case in point. Styron set out to write "a meditation on [the] history" of the abortive slave revolt led by Nat Turner in Virginia in 1831. Virtually the only source material available was the actual "confession" transcribed by a white lawyer in Turner's prison cell.

Styron's book was widely praised by white reviewers and won the Pulitzer Prize for fiction. But black writers were incensed by the novel. Their criticism was recently gathered together and published in a book called *William Styron's Nat Turner—Ten Black Writers Respond*. They contended that Styron had (1) failed to recognize the role played in Turner's upbringing by a black father and grandmother; (2) distorted Turner's sex life by focusing his desires on a white girl; and (3) portrayed Turner as incompetent during the revolt. The over-all effect of the novel, the black writers contended, was to perpetuate the stereotype of the bumbling slave dependent on his white masters.

Black Pride

Newly available textbooks, both original works and reprints of older books, make a point of mentioning such Negroes as Dr. Charles Drew, who was largely responsible for the development of blood plasma; Mathew Henson, who accompanied Peary all the way to the North Pole in 1909; and Elijah McCoy, a 19th century inventor who held more than 75 patents for mechanical devices and is believed to have inspired the expression "the real McCoy." Some educators have expressed concern, however, that the effort to give Negroes their due in American history texts may lead to distortion. There is some question whether Deadwood Dick, the legendary frontier cowboy, actually was a Negro, as is often claimed today. Similarly, many educators balk at the effort to glorify Crispus Attucks, a Negro or part-Negro reputed to have been the first person killed in the Boston Massacre and thus, by extension, in the American Revolution. Eyewitness accounts of the event lend support to the view that Attucks actually was one of a mob of ruffians who provoked the British troops into firing at them.

DEMANDS FOR BLACK CULTURE COURSES AT COLLEGE

Militant black student organizations on both Negro and white college campuses have demanded, often successfully, that courses in Negro history and culture be added to the curriculum. Harvard announced in June that, beginning in the 1968-69 college year, it would offer a full-year course in "The Afro-American Experience" and that it was considering a degree-granting program in Afro-American studies at a later date. The university said that the first term of the new course would deal with African background and the Negro experience in American history through 1945; the second term would consider issues of race relations, psychology, civil rights, housing, employment and education from 1945 to the present.

A joint student-faculty committee at Yale drafted a proposal last spring urging creation of a divisional major in Afro-American studies by September 1969. The *Yale Alumni Magazine* summarized the arguments favoring inclusion of black studies in the curriculum as follows:

> The present ignorance about the black experience has resulted in a lack of viable intellectual approaches to the racial crisis in this country. Colleges and universities, as mirrors of society at large, are in danger of becoming exclusively oriented toward white, middle-class values to the exclusion of other areas of experience. If they continue to follow the same course in the future as in the past, they

141

will only be acting to perpetuate the current racial situation by conveying a subtle bias to white students and by failing to allow black students to develop any sense of identity, purpose or direction.[30]

Such developments are by no means confined to private, Ivy League colleges. The National Endowment for the Humanities on July 17 gave $10,000 to each of seven colleges and universities [31] to hold summer workshops in Negro history and culture. The purpose of the workshops was to introduce college and university faculty members to published, unpublished, and graphic materials which would enable them to improve their instruction in the heritage of the American Negro and of his contributions to American life and culture.

The fact that many local school boards and college administrations have accepted Negro demands for courses in Afro-American culture attests in some measure to the reality of "black power." In time, these courses may help to enhance Negro self-esteem and to reshape white attitudes toward black Americans. Progress toward that end no doubt will be difficult, as in the past, but the crucial first steps are being taken.

[30] "Yale Takes First Step Toward a Major in Afro-American Studies," *Yale Alumni Magazine*, June 1968, p. 12.

[31] Boston University; Cazenovia College, Cazenovia, N. Y.; Duke University; Fisk University, Nashville; Howard University, Washington, D. C.; Morgan State University, Baltimore; Southern University, Baton Rouge, La.

PROTECTION OF THE ENVIRONMENT

by

Helen B. Shaffer

1 9 6 8
June 19

PROTECTION OF THE ENVIRONMENT

A MULTI-NATION EFFORT to tackle what is potentially the most serious of all problems facing mankind—deterioration of the human environment—is slowly getting into gear. The International Biological Program, to which 55 nations have pledged cooperation, is short on funds but long on hope that scientists all over the globe, working together or in complementary endeavors, will find a way to rescue the earth from the depredations of man before those depredations threaten his very survival. American scientists in the program are particularly interested in the environment-protection phase of the program because the United States, as the richest and most technologically advanced nation, does the lion's share of the contaminating.

Even as scientists began to draw up their I.B.P. study plans, they realized that, no matter how successful their studies, no good would result unless people and their governments became sufficiently concerned to take the steps necessary to maintain the earth's natural hospitality to man. The United States has been slow to move against the mounting menace. As Walter R. Hibbard Jr., director of the U. S. Bureau of Mines, said recently: "We respond to alarms only when the house is already on fire." [1]

RESULTS OF TARDY REACTION TO POLLUTION ABUSES

It took the killer smogs of Los Angeles and then New York to force action against the menace of airborne pollutants whose toxic effects were known before the situation became critical. Lake Erie "died" as a medium for living organisms before serious attention was given to protecting the Great Lakes. Recent federal anti-pollution legislation was enacted only after contamination of air, soil and waterways had become serious and widespread. Scientists and conservationists had been warning for many years that this would be the result if the abuses continued. Now, however,

---

[1] Walter R. Hibbard Jr., "Mineral Resources: Challenge or Threat?" *Science*, April 12, 1968, p. 143.

there appears to be growing appreciation within the United States and other advanced nations of the need for a broader, preventive approach to protection of the environment.[2]

Meanwhile, there is concern lest the underdeveloped countries, in their eagerness to take great strides toward a technology-based economy, will repeat and compound the environment-damaging mistakes of the advanced nations. It has been reported that I.B.P.-participating scientists from the poor countries have evinced prime interest in the phase of the International Biological Program that has to do with augmenting productivity. Their interest is natural in view of the difficulty these countries face in providing sufficient food for their rapidly growing populations, and in view of their hunger for other consumer goods as well. But if their efforts to boost productivity in agriculture and industry should follow the old route of indifference to the effects on the environment, the consequences for all mankind might be devastating.

FEAR OF IRREPARABLE DAMAGE TO THE BIOSPHERE

The threat of environmental deterioration goes well beyond the familiar difficulties with contaminated air and water. The basic concern is the combined effect of all changes wrought by man on the natural world. The changes include not only the discharge of poisons and other pollutants into the air, water and soil, but also the digging, blasting and leveling of land, the re-routing of waters, the covering-over of vegetation, the deliberate elimination of certain plants and animals deemed a nuisance to man—in short, all the things done to the natural environment in the name of civilization and economic progress.

Some scientists say these manifold man-made interferences with nature might irreparably damage the entire biosphere—the relatively thin layer of soil, water and air that supports life on earth. The grimmest of the prospects is that the changes wrought by modern man in his natural habitat might render it totally uninhabitable.

What causes fear is the possible results of man's intrusion on natural ecosystems—that is, the natural patterns of in-

---

[2] Major federal environment-protection laws include the Clean Air Act and Federal Water Pollution Control Act of 1963; the Motor Vehicle Air Pollution Control Act, Solid Waste Disposal Act, and Water Quality Act of 1965; the Clean Waters Restoration Act of 1966; and the Air Quality Act of 1967. See *Congressional Quarterly Almanac* for 1963 (pp. 236-241); 1965 (pp. 743-750 and 780-786); 1966 (pp. 685-687); and 1967 (pp. 1006-1009).

terrelationships between various animal and plant forms and between them and their environment. These relationships are basic to the maintenance of a life-supporting habitat. Explaining why he believes "continued pollution of the earth, if unchecked, will eventually destroy the fitness of this planet as a place for human life," Barry Commoner, director of the Center for Biology of Natural Systems at Washington University, St. Louis, wrote:

> The environment is a complex, subtly balanced system, and it is this integrated whole which receives the impact of all the separate insults inflicted by the pollutants. Never before in the history of this planet has its thin life-supporting surface been subjected to such diverse, novel, and potent agents. I believe the cumulative effects of these pollutants, their interactions and amplifications, can be fatal to the complex fabric of the biosphere.[3]

Other respected scientists in the various fields have voiced similar fears.

EMPHASIS ON ECOLOGY AS KEY TO MAN'S FUTURE

Scientific concern for the future of the human environment has given new prominence to ecology as a branch of scientific learning vital to the survival of man. Ecology as a distinct science is scarcely a century old, but it has ancient forebears in the study of natural science. It is essentially a multiple discipline, calling on the findings of a number of biological and physical sciences. Some knowledge of ecology is essential to modern agriculture, and ecological findings have been a main support of the conservation movement in the United States since its founding in the late 19th century. But only recently has ecology's urgent application to man's fate come forward. Ecologists in general still feel that the public has not altogether awakened to the full import of the connection.

In an address before the American Association for the Advancement of Science on Dec. 27, 1967, LaMont C. Cole, professor of ecology at Cornell University, complained that ecologists had failed to deliver their prime message, which "could hardly be more urgent or important." The message was simply that man "in the process of seeking 'a better way of life' is destroying the natural environment that is essential to any kind of human life at all."

There are some indications that the worries of ecologists are beginning to seep into public consciousness and to affect

[3] Barry Commoner, *Science and Survival* (1966), pp. 110-111.

public policy on environmental protection. The Conservation Foundation recently commented that "Everyone's getting into the ecological act." It noted that new offices of ecology had been established by the Department of the Interior and the Smithsonian Institution, that the U. S. Army Corps of Engineers had appointed an environmental planning board, and that the National Academy of Sciences and the National Academy of Engineering had jointly established an Environmental Studies Board.[4]

The first scientist to succeed in winning a wide popular audience for the ecologists' crusade against injudicious interferences by man in the natural environment was the late Rachel Carson, a marine biologist with unusual gifts as a writer. In her best-selling book *The Silent Spring* (1962), Miss Carson attacked what she considered excessive and indiscriminate use of pesticides and the acquiescence of the government in this practice. She stressed not only the danger to human health from direct contamination, but also the potentially damaging effects of widespread spraying of chemical poisons on the life-supporting character of the earthly environment.

Miss Carson's book stirred up considerable controversy. Although she was described in some quarters as an alarmist, later developments vindicated her broad concept of the nature of the environmental hazard. Several influential government-sponsored studies in the years following publication of *The Silent Spring* reflected similar broad concern over the impact of man's mistreatment of his environment on its ecological stability. The influence of these studies is apparent in the unprecedented flow of anti-pollution legislation enacted by Congress in the past few years.

WARNINGS ON ECOLOGICAL EFFECTS OF POLLUTION

The Environmental Pollution Panel of the President's Science Advisory Committee reported in 1965 on a study it had made of the entire pollution problem. In a 316-page book published under the White House imprint with a foreword by President Johnson, the panel of eminent scientists emphasized the ecological factor, noting that "plants provide the principal mechanism whereby energy from the sun can serve the earth's inhabitants" and thus "maintain the oxygen of the air and furnish the basic habitat and foods of animals and men."

---

[4] Conservation Foundation newsletter, Feb. 23, 1968.

Because living things are interdependent and interacting, they form a complex, dynamic system. Tampering with this system may be desirable and necessary, as in agriculture. . . . But such tampering often produces unexpected results, or side effects, and these are sometimes very damaging. Many of the effects of pollution fall into this category. . . . Many kinds of pollution problems could be prevented by the exercise of ecological foresight.

The panel urged that in the future "advance evaluations" of ecological effects be made before particular pollutants were cast into the environment.[5]

A broad view of the whole complex problem of environmental protection was taken by a Committee on Pollution set up by the National Academy of Sciences-National Research Council. In a report issued in 1966, this expert group described the problem in terms of man's wastes. "Pollutants," the committee said, "are the residues of the things we make, use and throw away." Man has only three ways of getting rid of his throw-aways: bury them, cast them into the waters, or burn them (in effect, releasing them into the atmosphere). The committee stressed the fact that the three natural disposal elements—soil, water and air—had limited capacities to perform this function. If overloaded, they would deteriorate; if the pollution load became too great, they might even cease to serve as sustainers of life.

The report laid special stress on the unpredictable nature of man-made disturbances of ecosystems, which "comprise the interacting living and non-living elements in a particular habitat." It asserted that "Until we understand man as an ecological agent (as man in nature), and not what man does to, or gets back from nature, we will not have any sure guiding principles." It was extremely important, therefore, to study the "whole environment of man" if the pollution problem was to be solved.[6]

CALL FOR U. S. COUNCIL OF ECOLOGICAL ADVISERS

A task force on environmental health set up by the Department of Health, Education, and Welfare reported in 1967 that there was a need in government for expert guidance on over-all policy affecting the environment. It recommended that the President ask Congress to approve establishment of a Council of Ecological Advisers "to provide an

---

[5] President's Science Advisory Committee, Environmental Pollution Panel, *Restoring the Quality of Our Environment* (November 1965), pp. 5, 14.

[6] National Academy of Sciences-National Research Council, *Waste Management and Control* (1966), p. 38.

overview, to assess activities in both the public and private
sectors affecting environmental change, . . . to advise on
critical environmental risk-benefit decisions; and . . . to be
instrumental in the shaping of national policy on environmental management." The task force said it was of "utmost
importance" that the President have "constant, well-in-
formed advice and program coordination" if the environment were to be adequately protected.[7]

Sens. Henry M. Jackson (D Wash.), Thomas H. Kuchel
(R Calif.) and Gaylord Nelson (D Wis.) and Reps. John D.
Dingell (D Mich.), John V. Tunney (D Calif.), and Spark
M. Matsunaga (D Hawaii) are among sponsors of pending
bills to create the proposed Council of Ecological Advisers.
Supporters of the proposal see the council as a small body of
impartial experts advising the government on ecological
questions in much the same way that the Council of Economic Advisers serves the President on economic matters.
An ecological council would not only help the government to
coordinate its many separate environment protection programs; it would also give consideration to the effect on the
environment of damaging or potentially damaging activities
all over the country.

Sen. Edmund S. Muskie (D Maine), with 19 co-sponsors,
has introduced a resolution to establish in the Senate a Select
Committee on Technology and the Human Environment, so
that the Senate would have its own means of "learning more
about the problems caused by advancing technology and
about the ways that science and technology can provide solutions to these problems." Muskie said he was moved to advance this proposal by the testimony of experts indicating
the complexity of the problem and the seriousness of its implications for man; he quoted the following statement by
Assistant Surgeon General James A. Shannon, director of
the National Institutes of Health:

> At the moment of our great victories over many . . . diseases . . . ,
> we are now confronted with the realization that the most formidable
> and pervasive challenges to the well-being of man lie in . . . the
> hazards man has created for himself in the products, processes, and
> living patterns of his increasingly technological world.[8]

The proposed select committee would consider problems
ranging from air and water pollution to the psychological

[7] Department of Health, Education, and Welfare Task Force on Environmental
Health and Related Problems, *A Strategy for a Livable Environment*, June 1967.

[8] Quoted by Sen. Muskie, U. S. Senate, Jan. 25, 1967.

stresses of urban living. The committee's life would be limited to a three-year period, at the end of which it would render a comprehensive report. A similar proposal to establish a "technology assessment board" to assist Congress has been introduced in the House by Rep. Emilio Q. Daddario (D Conn.).

CONGRESSIONAL INTEREST; U.S.P.H.S. REORGANIZATION

Congressional interest in the broader aspects of the environmental problem is evident also in resolutions introduced by Rep. Daddario and Rep. George P. Mieler (D Calif.) endorsing the International Biological Program and calling on government agencies, private groups and citizens to support that program. Daddario, who is chairman of a science and research subcommittee, scheduled a one-day hearing in May 1967 for routine review and approval of the relatively simple I.B.P. resolution. When the subcommittee reported nearly a year later, it said it had found that "while the resolution was simple, . . . the I.B.P. and the problems it represents could not [be readily disposed of]."

> As the hearings progressed intermittently through the summer, it became ever more clear . . . that the I.B.P. was not just another international cooperative . . . program. It dealt, on the contrary, with one of the most crucial situations to face this or any other civilization—the immediate or near potential of man to damage, perhaps beyond repair, the ecological system of the planet, on which all life depends.[9]

"Evidence of growing congressional concern over ecological problems is clearly at hand," the report said. For the most part, the concern showed up with relation to "seemingly isolated problems—pollution, food resources, wilderness conservation, water use, etc.—rather than with total ecosystems." But there was growing recognition of the fact that "the nation will eventually have to deal with the latter in order to handle the former."

An impending reorganization within the U. S. Public Health Service may encourage broader consideration of environmental probems as they relate to human health. The President announced on June 15 that he had approved a plan to consolidate a number of U.S.P.H.S. units to form an over-all agency to be known as the Consumer Protection and Environmental Health Service. The new agency will absorb

---

[9] House Committee on Science and Astronautics, Subcommittee on Science, Research and Development, *The International Biological Program: Its Meaning and Needs*, March 11, 1968, p. 2.

the Food and Drug Administration and the National Centers for Air Pollution Control, Radiological Health, Urban and Industrial Health, and (in part) Communicable Disease. It will begin functioning on July 1, 1968. Responsibility for carrying out the reorganization was assigned to Secretary of Health, Education, and Welfare Wilbur J. Cohen, who was named chief adviser to the President on health policy. Cohen is planning to form an interdepartmental health council to perform the advisory function.

Shape of Threats to the Environment

HOW SERIOUS is the environmental situation? Nearly everyone agrees that there is an environmental "crisis," but some are more gloomy than others on the prospects of solving the problem. When President Johnson signed the Air Quality Act, Nov. 21, 1967, he quoted from Dante's *Inferno* —"Dirty water and black snow pour from the dismal air to . . . the putrid slush . . ."—and then asked, "Isn't it a forecast that fits almost any large American city?" In similar vein, Secretary of Agriculture Orville L. Freeman, addressing the Agriculture and Natural Resources Committee of the U. S. Chamber of Commerce on Feb. 2, 1968, quoted as follows from a new book by one of a number of authors who have cried havoc at the state of the environment: "When some future historian shall sit down to summarize what the present generation of Americans has accomplished, his climactic sentence could read: 'Of the waters, they made a cesspool; of the air, a depository for poisons; and of the good earth itself, a dump. . . .' " [10]

VOLUME OF POLLUTANTS IN THE AIR AND WATER

Statistics on the amount of contamination have been compiled; calculations on the consequences and potential consequences, and especially on the full ecological effects, of contamination are much less precise. The President said at the bill-signing ceremony last November that "We are pouring at least 130 million tons of poison into the air each year . . . two-thirds of a ton for every man, woman and child in America." The director of the U. S. Public Health Service's

---

[10] George R. Stewart, *Not So Rich As You Think* (1968), p. 1.

National Center for Urban and Industrial Health, Jerome H. Svore, testified recently that an average of five pounds of waste per person is being thrown away every day, "much of it threatening health by polluting the air when it is burned or befouling our land and water through dumping." [11]

The load is bound to increase with population growth. The H.E.W. task force predicted that "the 165 million tons of solid waste spewed into the air . . . in 1966 will increase to 260 million tons in little more than a decade," while the number of scrapped automobiles—six million in 1965—will "double, perhaps triple, before the year 2000." Aside from total volume increase, the disposal problem is expected to worsen because an increasing proportion of the wastes will be non-degradable inorganic material; the proportion of such material is already 65 per cent.

The effect of the growing pollution load on fresh water supplies was summed up last year by Dr. Glenn T. Seaborg, chairman of the Atomic Energy Commission: "By 1980 we will be producing enough sewage and other waterborne wastes to consume, in dry weather, all the oxygen in all 22 river systems of the United States. Yet our need for clean, fresh water . . . will rise in 20 years [from 370 billion gallons per day] to over 600 billion gallons per day." [12]

WIDE VARIETY IN THE SOURCES OF CONTAMINATION

In addition to such predictable loads, there are accidents which inflict unexpected assaults on the environment. The running aground of the tanker *Torrey Canyon* off the coast of England on March 18, 1967, was a grim reminder of a worldwide hazard. The spill of crude oil from the 120,000-ton tanker blackened miles of coast and caused the death of sea birds. This disaster also pointed up the dangers in certain of man's responses to environmental crises. A British scientific report found that the use of detergents to disperse oil on Cornish beaches had proved even more lethal to marine life than the oil.[13] Threats of this kind to shore lands and coastal waters—to say nothing of ocean ecosystems— are augmented by a trend toward much larger tankers than the *Torrey Canyon*. Growing appreciation of the pollution threat from seagoing vessels in general inspired bills now

---

[11] Testimony, House Appropriations subcommittee, March 12, 1968.

[12] Testimony, Senate Government Operations Subcommittee on Intergovernmental Relations, March 20, 1967.

[13] "Pollution: The Wake of the 'Torrey Canyon,'" *Science*, April 12, 1968, p. 167. The finding on the detergents was made by the Marine Biological Association of the United Kingdom.

pending in Congress to require federal regulation of discharges from ship and shore installations.[14]

The variety of environmental hazards which crop up unexpectedly appears endless. Some years ago concern over excess radiation led to the removal from stores of X-ray machines used in fitting shoes for children. Last year the government found that a number of color television sets in use emitted more than a desirable amount of radiation. Set manufacturers promised to correct the flaw in new models. Meanwhile, though the amount of emitted radiation was small even on faulty sets, the U. S. Public Health Service suggested that children not be allowed to sit too close to the TV screen.

The President in a message to Congress on consumer interests, Feb. 6, 1968, asked for legislation to require that all electronic products meet radiation safety standards. Several bills to that effect are under consideration. Dr. Allen V. Astin, director of the National Bureau of Standards, testified before the Senate Commerce Committee on May 8, 1968, that "Evidence of existing or potential hazard [from electronic products] . . . clearly indicates the need for . . . more effective safeguards for the public."

Use of vast quantities of pesticides to maintain agricultural productivity (and to keep homes and home gardens free of pests) is viewed by some ecologists as the most devastating of all forms of environmental pollution. The U. S. Department of Agriculture has at last recognized the hazards of DDT by reducing its own spraying with this chemical to some 100,000 acres, compared with 4.9 million acres in 1957. But DDT is still said to be the most widely used pesticide in the world.

DDT is a chlorinated hydrocarbon, which does not break down easily; it has an estimated half-life of approximately 10 years. On this basis, an ecologist has deduced that "more than a billion pounds [of DDT] must now be available to the earth's biota [flora and fauna]," and that if present levels of use continue, the amount will double in 50 years.[15] DDT residues have been found in animals, including man, in every part of the globe—Eskimos and Antarctic penguins, for ex-

---

[14] Other provisions of pending water pollution control legislation deal with acid pollution of waterways from mines. See *Congressional Quarterly Weekly Report*, May 10, 1968, pp. 1045-1047.

[15] G. M. Woodwell, Brookhaven National Laboratory, letter, *Washington Post*, June 2, 1968.

ample—indicating the wide range of the pesticide's ecological effects. DDT is particularly deadly to marine life, accounting for declining populations and for the expected extinction of ocean-scavenging birds like the Bermuda petrel. Ecologists are profoundly concerned over the unknown ultimate effects of disturbances in the ecology of the oceans when a natural predator is artificially removed from the food chain.

POSSIBILITY OF DEATH-DEALING LOSSES OF OXYGEN

There are many pessimists among ecologists today, and LaMont C. Cole, Cornell professor and president of the Ecology Society of America, may well be their champion. His address before the American Association for the Advancement of Science last December projected a number of dire possibilities in man's future. One of them was death-dealing loss of oxygen from the atmosphere.

It has long been recognized that burning of fossil fuels is adding carbon dioxide to the earth's atmosphere. The Environmental Pollution Panel of the President's Science Advisory Committee reported that man was burning coal, oil, and natural gas at the rate of six billion tons a year; at that rate and with the growth of population, the amount of carbon dioxide in the air was expected to increase by one-fourth over the remainder of the century. "This will modify the heat balance of the atmosphere to such an extent that marked changes in climate, not controllable through local or even national efforts, could occur," the panel reported.

A possible result of the carbon dioxide increase would be a warming of the earth sufficient to melt the Antarctic ice cap, which in turn would raise sea levels by 400 feet. Even if the melting took place over a thousand years, the panel said, it would still mean a rise of four feet every 10 years. The result would be inundation of major cities. Other scientists believe that the temperature change would cause enough precipitation to loosen the ice cap and launch a new ice age.

Cole envisioned an even more depressing possibility in the increase of carbon dioxide. He suggested that it would be accompanied by a decline in the amount of oxygen because of a reduction of plant photosynthesis due to the paving over of green plant acreage. Nearly one million acres are lost to photosynthesis in this way every year in the United

155

States alone, Cole estimated. "And we do not even know to what extent we are inhibiting photosynthesis through pollution of fresh-water and marine environments." The result was that "the carbon-oxygen balance is tipping," and "when, and if, we reach the point at which the rate of combustion exceeds the rate of photosynthesis, we shall start running out of oxygen." [16]

VAST UNKNOWNS IN DETERIORATION OF ENVIRONMENT

Such speculation is possible because no one really knows what the total impact of man's activities will have on the capacity of his environment to support him in the future. "So much of the danger to man is summed up in that simple phrase, 'We don't know,' " wrote Cole. Even on the question of the effects on individual health of direct exposure to pollutants, there are great blanks of knowledge. "We do not have today the kind of numbers that we should have in order to determine what is a hazard in the environment and what is a safe level of exposure, whether . . . in our water supplies or food or in the air," Svore told a House Appropriations subcommittee on March 12. ". . . . We are creating new chemicals to put into our environments at a very rapid rate and we do not know what their toxicology is."

There are so many unknowns—the effect of weather modification measures, for example. It has been suggested also that "increasing jet travel may be altering the atmospheric radiation processes." [17] Dr. Frederick Smith of the University of Michigan has listed the following phenomena which suggest that insidious changes for the worse may be taking place in the environment aside from the obvious effects of water and air pollution—such changes as "the thinning of the soil, the increasing need to spray crops, the increasing abundance of weeds, the dense algal blooms in lakes, the decreasing abundance of sport fish, and the changes in species of birds in our towns." [18] These changes, which take place over long periods of time, are difficult to document, Smith said, and difficult to get action on. "Many of these problems are deeply rooted in ecological systems.

[16] LaMont C. Cole, "Can the World Be Saved?" (adapted from address to American Association for the Advancement of Science, Dec. 27, 1967), *New York Times Magazine*, March 31, 1968, p. 95.

[17] "Climate Control," *Physics Today*, August 1967, p. 30.

[18] *Analysis of Ecosystems* (proposal to National Science Foundation), January 1968, quoted in House Science and Astronautics Subcommittee on Science, Research, and Development report, *The International Biological Program: Its Meaning and Needs* (March 11, 1968), p. 9.

They are system responses in which the visible effect appears in one part of the system while the cause lies in another."

Man is recognized as a highly adaptable creature, as his survival over the past million years or so would testify. According to Dr. Frederick Sargent II, another leading ecologist, man's ability to survive today in the "complex urban agglomerations characterized by crowding, deteriorating habitations, and pollution from noise, heat, dust, dirt and chemicals" is itself evidence of his great adaptive power. But this remarkable faculty has limits, and man's past history, said Dr. Sargent, offers no basis for reliably predicting that the human race can survive in such a "novel environment" as the one he is now "nonchalantly creating" for his future. Environmental changes in the past took place slowly, giving time for adaptation through genetic selectivity. "Because the pace of environmental change has accelerated, he [man] may not have enough time for evolutionary modifications." [19]

Action Aimed to Protect Environment

SCIENCE and technology, the two great benefactors of modern man which are responsible also for many of his environmental problems, are now being looked to for solution of those problems: science to provide knowledge of what should be done, technology to provide the means of keeping the earth habitable. Major anti-pollution laws adopted by Congress over the past five years have provided new funds and other incentives to research and development, as well as setting up new machinery for enforcing clean air and water standards. The Committee on Environmental Quality of the Federal Council for Science and Technology estimated recently that the federal government will have spent $251 million in the year ending June 30, 1968, for pollution research, development, and demonstration. The data were drawn from no less than 30 separate agencies of government.

In a special message on conservation, March 8, 1968,

---

[19] Frederick Sargent II, M.D. (professor of Human Ecology at the University of Wisconsin, Green Bay, and chairman of the Subcommittee on Human Adaptability of the U. S. National Committee for the International Biological Program), "The Adaptability of Man," *Medical Opinion and Review*, March 1968, p. 38.

President Johnson asked Congress to commit $475 million
to help pay off municipal bonds issued for construction of
waste treatment plants. The $475 million would be in addi-
tion to $225 million requested for construction of sewage
treatment facilities in the regular budget for fiscal 1969,
submitted to Congress on Jan. 29, 1968. Measures to authorize the additional assistance are now pending before Congress. The Federal Water Pollution Control Administration
in the Interior Department had submitted a report a few
days earlier in which it estimated that cleansing of the
nation's waterways of municipal and industrial wastes
would cost $26 billion to $29 billion over the next five years.

Grants to states and communities for air pollution control
became available under legislation enacted in 1965. An estimated $33 million has been spent in the fiscal year ending
June 30, 1968, on grants for research, fellowships, training,
control programs, and surveys and demonstrations. John T.
Middleton, director of the National Center for Air Pollution
Control, reported on March 11, 1968, that state, regional and
local air pollution control budgets had increased 82 per cent
since the federal grants became available. But the current
level of activity still represented only half of what Middleton felt was needed "to attain a reasonably effective degree
of air pollution control." [20]

A total of $32.2 million has been appropriated over the
past two years under the Solid Waste Disposal Act of 1965,
much of it for research and development. Among new pol-
lution-reducing devices being tested are a sanitary landfill
machine which excavates, deposits refuse, and applies soil
cover in a single operation, an incinerator designed to hold
down emission of pollutants, and a machine developed in
Japan that compresses wastes into building blocks. The
government is studying the feasibility of using pipelines to
collect solid wastes and deliver them to abandoned mines or
use them as fill in mine strippings.

RACE BETWEEN ABATEMENT AND NEW DETERIORATION

The race between abatement technology and despoliation
is close. Some authorities think that environmental deterioration is well ahead of measures to prevent it. "With advancing technology," Jerome H. Svore testified, ". . . problems are being created faster than we can solve them. This

---

[20] Testimony, House Appropriations subcommittee, March 11, 1968.

is true in many areas of the environment, whether it is in water supply or in matters of sanitation."

Conservationists often complain of too much dependence on technology. The building of cities and suburbs on fertile land, followed by diversion of waters to irrigate arid lands, is often cited as a case in point. Nor is irrigation always successful. "Unless great care is taken," wrote Cole, "irrigation can . . . ruin land" by drawing salt-laden water to the surface. According to Secretary of Agriculture Freeman, about one-half of the 32 million acres of irrigated land in 17 western states is subject to salinization, including acreage in California which grows 40 per cent of the nation's fruit and vegetables. "Some irrigated lands in the Southwest have registered up to 25 tons of salt per acre-foot of water used," Freeman said.[21]

The heavy use of chemical fertilizers, which greatly increased agricultural productivity but were carried by runoff to streams where they killed fish, afforded another instance of an ecological backfire. Similarly, extensive use of pesticides encouraged the proliferation of resistant strains or poisoned the food of natural predators that were friends of the farmer. "Man is a simplifier of complex ecosystems," writes Prof. Paul Ehrlich of Stanford University. An ecosystem thrives when it is complex, has many interchangeable parts, and a large gene pool to assure adaptation to changing conditions. "Synthetic pesticides are one of man's potent tools for reducing the complexity of ecosystems," said Dr. Ehrlich.[22]

Now there is foreboding over the prospect that the problem of wastes from burning of fossil fuels will be "solved" by the substitution of nuclear power installations. The beginnings of such a movement are already here. But what of the problem of disposing of radioactive wastes? John P. Milton of the Conservation Foundation points out that "The United States has stored them in concrete blocks and buried them in the ocean, in caves, salt domes and deep wells." And he asks: "What are the risks from this process of groundwater contamination, especially in earthquake zones where vertical shearing of strata may take place?" [23] There may be

[21] Address, Agriculture and Natural Resources Committee of U. S. Chamber of Commerce, Washington, D. C., Feb. 2, 1968.

[22] Address, Palo Alto, May 7, 1968, from forthcoming book, *Population Control.*

[23] John P. Milton, *Resources in America: The Coming Crisis* (Population Reference Bureau, Selection No. 23, May 1968), p. 4.

also some risk of release of radioactive materials into the ocean through container decomposition.

PLANS FOR THE INTERNATIONAL BIOLOGICAL PROGRAM

It is obvious that to protect the environment fully, much more basic scientific knowledge must be obtained on the functioning of the various ecosystems, the effect on them of sundry natural and man-made forces, and, above all, how modern man in a technological world still fits into the total biological picture.

Much hope for obtaining that knowledge rests with plans for the International Biological Program, a five-year project which moved into its "action phase" in July 1967 after three years of planning.[24]

Each of the 55 participating countries has a national committee to review research project proposals. The U. S. National Committee was originally headed by Dr. Richard Revelle, director of Harvard University's Population Center, who was succeeded by Dr. W. Frank Blair of the University of Texas, former president of the Ecological Society of America. At least 5,000 American scientists are expected to participate in the program. The federal government became a participant in late 1965, after the Federal Council for Science and Technology had concluded that "the resources, facilities and staff of the federal agencies" should be involved in the program. The council designated the National Science Foundation as the coordinating agency for federal participation. An Interagency Coordinating Committee was then formed to facilitate the federal effort.

So far, Congress has made no direct financial contribution to the program, but combined contributions by participating federal agencies have averaged around $300,000 a year. Promoters of I.B.P. in Congress have not pressed for larger funding because of the long time required to prepare for the research projects, but a direct appropriation is expected to be sought in the 91st Congress. It has been estimated that the United States phase of the program will require about $4 million for the first year of research and training, and between $30 million and $50 million for the full five-year period.

I.B.P. planners expect the research projects to be of such

---

[24] The idea of an international biological program was conceived in 1959 in conversations between leaders of the International Council of Scientific Unions and the International Union of Biological Sciences. I.B.P. was formally established in 1964.

magnitude and importance that the studies will be continued after the scheduled five-year "action phase" ends in July 1972. It is hoped that by that time the pattern of international cooperation and coordination of research on problems of such universal importance will be well established. The Daddario committee report described the nature of the over-all program as follows:

> The international biological program is a global plan of environmental research (basic and applied) designed specifically to make a broad and telling contribution to human welfare. Convinced that we are living and operating in a major state of ignorance about the crucial inter-relationships between people and their environment, the I.B.P. has evolved prototype concepts and guidelines of radical scientific sweep. In seeking answers of paramount importance to man's survival, the program will indirectly develop the fledgling discipline of ecosystematics—the principles and processes of large environments in their totality (man, vegetation, climate, soils, and animals).[25]

The problem of controlling population growth by reducing births is not on the agenda. American scientists believe that this problem is central to the maintenance of a tolerable environment; others in the program put more stress on increasing productivity to feed the growing populations.

Checking over-population by chemical control of fertility is no longer a scientific problem, pointed out Prof. Jean Baer of Neuchatel University in Switzerland, president of the Special Committee for the I.B.P. That solution is "beyond the power of scientists to apply, belonging as it does to the realm of ethics and politics." [26] In a sense, the same is true of all environmental protection measures. The scientists say they are looking for the answers; after that, it's up to the people to decide if they can afford to ignore the facts.

[25] House Committee on Science and Astronautics, Subcommittee on Science, Research and Development, *The International Biological Program: Its Meaning and Needs,* March 11, 1968, p. 49.

[26] Jean Baer, "Biology and Humanity: The International Biological Programme," *Impact of Science on Society,* Vol. VII, 1967, p. 316.

NEW TOWNS

by

Hoyt Gimlin

1 9 6 8
Nov. 6

NEW TOWNS

E VERY YEAR a million acres of American countryside succumb to the bulldozer to meet the needs of an expanding urban population. Public figures are predicting that for every building now standing another will be added by the turn of the century, only a generation away. Robert C. Weaver, the Secretary of Housing and Urban Development, has pointed out that "Regardless of the merits or defects of our present suburbs, we shall see more of them." [1] The question, he says, is not whether to encourage more housing development in the fringe areas and beyond, but whether to go about it in more creative ways and make the new dwelling places more economical and more attractive.

Construction of "new towns" is proposed as a means of satisfying the housing demand and at the same time providing havens for refugees from the racial ghettos of big cities. But there is general agreement that new towns—cities built from scratch according to a single master plan—can perform such an exalted social and esthetic function only if aided by federal funds and planning. The President's Council on Recreation and Natural Beauty, headed by Hubert H. Humphrey, has just recommended to President Johnson that a wide variety of federal resources be made available, at least on a trial basis, to help private builders assemble land and to guarantee the necessary long-term financing for their development. This proposal for federally aided land acquisition is one of the strongest statements of support for new towns that has come from a governmental group.[2]

The Advisory Commission on Intergovernmental Relations made similar recommendations Nov. 3 in a report titled

---

[1] Robert C. Weaver, *Dilemmas of Urban America* (1965), p. 8.

[2] The council is composed of the Secretaries of Defense, Interior, Agriculture, Commerce, Health, Education and Welfare, Housing and Urban Development, and Transportation; the chairmen of the Federal Power Commission and the Tennessee Valley Authority; and the heads of the General Services Administration and the Bureau of Outdoor Recreation. The council's 304-page report, *From Sea to Shining Sea*, was issued Oct. 26, 1968.

Urban and Rural America: Policies for Future Growth. The commission—composed of officials at the federal, state and local levels—said the building of entire new communities from the ground up offers a promising method of influencing the quality of urban growth. It suggested a wide variety of public assistance to new town development in the form of grants, loans, tax credits and tax deferrals.

RESTON AS PROTOTYPE OF SELF-CONTAINED CITY

Reston, Va., one of the showplaces of America's multiplying new towns, is now slowly rising alongside a man-made lake some 18 miles from downtown Washington; the plan calls for a community of 75,000 people by 1980. Clusters of apartments and colorful townhouses, stores and shops line the banks of the lake and form the central part of a "village." Six other villages, apart from one another but all within easy access of a town center that is designed to provide the amenities of city life, are to be built eventually.

Many village neighbors can walk to their shops without encountering a car; automobiles have been banished to outer roadways. Characteristic of the planning at Reston, the first specialist employed at the town site was not an engineer but a forester. The community was laid out with an eye to landscape and topography, on 7,400 acres of an old fox-hunting estate. Great slices of open space were set aside for woodland, lakes, playing fields and commons. Robert E. Simon Jr., the guiding hand of Reston's early development, scorned the "subdivider's mentality" [3] of scattering houses over an entire tract without reserving any ground for common use. "Cluster housing" permits equal, or even greater, density while leaving expanses of greenery intact.

Reston at this point has attracted 4,000 residents who prefer it to the close-in but cluttered suburbs. But this paradise, too, has its problems. Few of the residents work at Reston and many must commute daily to Washington through heavy traffic. Some visitors come away from the new town with the feeling that it smacks of paternalism and preciosity.

Urbanologists are asking if dwellers in new towns are showing the nation a better way of living—a way that will remove pressures from the overflowing big cities and arrest

---

[3] Interview in April 1967.

suburban sprawl. Or will the new towns do as the traditional suburbs have done, drain away the middle class from the central cities and leave behind poverty and segregation. The people who live in Reston tend to be young, of moderate to upper-middle income, and in the professions.

Reston might be merely a stylish country club district if on-site industry and jobs were not a part of its plan. The town has attracted about a dozen light industries so far and hopes to have enough eventually to employ 30 per cent of the community's wage-earners. At Reston's dedication in May 1966, Secretary of the Interior Stewart L. Udall said: "A true new town must be a cross-section of America and it must be deemed a failure, despite the brilliance of its design or the insight of community planning . . . if it is an enclave of the well-to-do or the private preserve of a single ethnic or racial group."

Udall has ordered the construction at Reston of a new headquarters for the U. S. Geological Survey, by 1972 if funds are available. The Geological Survey found recently that of its 2,800 employees who would be moved to Reston, 442 were eligible for low- and moderate-income housing subsidized by the federal government. So far, no such housing exists there. The Federal Housing Administration has approved 200 units at Reston for families too well off to qualify for public housing but too poor to afford non-subsidized housing,[4] but construction has been delayed because of county restrictions.

'INSTANT CITIES' OF MARYLAND AND CALIFORNIA

As many as 200 self-styled "new towns" or "new cities" or "new communities" of 5,000 or more acres, under construction or planned, have been counted from the Atlantic Coast to California. But only a handful of the towns seem to have serious aspirations of providing jobs as well as housing, and a balanced economy. Two of the most ambitious are Columbia, Md., and Irvine, Calif. Irvine is eight years into a 50-year plan to convert 88,000 acres of ranch land into a community of 500,000 people. It will occupy one-fifth of Orange County, southeast of Los Angeles. The master plan was drawn up by architect William L. Pereira, who was retained

---

[4] The subsidy takes the form of a low-cost government loan to the builder, who then rents to eligible tenants at 20 to 25 per cent below prevailing rates. To provide truly low-income housing, Reston holds a $240,000 grant from the Department of Housing and Urban Development for applying to on-site houses the techniques used in building house trailers.

by the University of California in 1959, originally to lay out a satellite campus for about 27,000 students on land donated by the Irvine Co. But Pereira proposed an entire university community which someday would occupy 10,000 acres, six times the size of the campus itself. The Irvine directors were so impressed that they asked him to extend his plans to embrace the whole ranch.

Columbia is being built on 13,690 acres of farmland in Howard County, Md., halfway between Baltimore and Washington. The acreage was assembled piecemeal, beginning in 1962, by James H. Rouse, a Baltimore investment banker and developer. The first residents moved in five years later. According to current projections, Columbia will have a population of 3,000 by the end of 1968 and of 110,000 to 125,000 when completed in the early 1980s. Rouse places less emphasis on quality of architecture than Simon did at Reston, but a liking for cluster development is found at both towns.

Rouse brought to his task a wide background in urban affairs. He was one of the framers of the Housing Act of 1954, which led to creation of the Urban Renewal Administration; he was a member of the Rockefeller Foundation's advisory committee on urban design and at present is chairman of Urban America, Inc., a non-profit organization aiming to improve the quality of urban life. Rouse has a reputation for combining aesthetics and profitability.

Rouse carefully placed Columbia at a point where the Washington and Baltimore suburbs almost come together. Those suburbs offer a large population base from which the new town may draw residents, and from which its stores may attract customers, before the town itself is fully developed. Unlike Reston, where the town center is still on the drawing board, Columbia's is already taking shape. An eight-story office building has been completed, another will go up soon, and a gigantic shopping center is rising along a mall that is to be enclosed. The Columbia management foresees 3,000 business and industrial jobs, exclusive of construction, in the town at the year's end. In October, Howard County commissioners approved plans for construction of a $250 million General Electric plant at Columbia. A General Electric spokesman said the company hoped to open the facility in 1971 with an initial work force of 2,000, eventually to be expanded to 12,000.

Two colleges are scheduled to open in Columbia in the autumn of 1970, the new Dag Hammarskjold liberal arts college and the two-year Howard County Community College. However, the colleges will not be a focal point of community development as the University of California campus is at Irvine. At both Columbia and Irvine, agricultural land will continue to be farmed until it is ready for development. This practice provides some needed revenue during the early stages and also gives the developers certain tax benefits.

BIG BUSINESS INVOLVEMENT IN NEW COMMUNITIES

The ultimate cost of building a new town is still largely conjectural, but some educated guesses have been offered. *Fortune* magazine estimated last year that the cost would run to $1 billion over a 20-year period; about a year earlier, *Business Week* had calculated the probable cost of building Columbia at $2 billion.[5] Whether one billion or two, only big business has the money, management talent, and staying power necessary in this kind of venture. A huge initial investment is required, with no return for several years. *Business Week* reported that Rouse expected to break even on his investment in Columbia in the fourth year of the town's operation (1970) and be debt-free in the tenth year.

Rouse's position is considered exceptionally good among new-town developers. He has obtained investment capital from the Connecticut General Life Insurance Co.,[6] the Teachers Insurance & Annuity Association, and the Chase Manhattan Bank. Gulf Oil Corp., an early backer of Reston, took over management of that project in the autumn of 1967. Housing sales had lagged in a tight-money market and Simon had run into financial difficulty. The name of the development corporation was changed from Reston, Inc. to Gulf Reston.

Other corporate giants involved in new towns include Humble Oil & Refining Co., which is building Clear Lake City 23 miles southeast of Houston, Texas, and Goodyear Tire & Rubber Co., which is developing a new community of Litchfield Park outside of Phoenix, Ariz. The list includes also such diverse companies as Walt Disney Productions,

---

[5] See "The Instant City," *Fortune*, June 1967, p. 135, and "Master Builder With a New Concept," *Business Week*, Aug. 20, 1966.

[6] A report to the stockholders of James W. Rouse & Co., Oct. 26, 1967, listed Connecticut General as 50 per cent owner of stock in Howard Research and Development Corp., the Rouse affiliate that owns and manages Columbia.

Kaiser Industries, and the American-Hawaiian Steamship Co. "In the long run each company expects to make a profit," *Fortune* commented, "but some of the new developers are also looking on their new towns as large-scale promotion." Southern California Edison intends to build an "all-electric" city west of Los Angeles; Westinghouse has said it will build in Florida a 10,000-acre new town where it can experiment with new products and systems, including urban transit, garbage disposal equipment, and home appliances. To demonstrate all that electricity can do, General Electric announced in 1966 that it too would launch a new town at a time and place as yet undisclosed.

FINANCIAL PROBLEMS AND FEDERAL ASSISTANCE

Housing and Home reported in June 1966 that the magazine's editors had found that new towns were meeting serious problems at almost every step from financing to sales. In the case of Reston, an architecture critic has observed, Simon spent six years creating it on "faith, hope and desperate, last-minute injections of cash." [7] Finally, when he was unable to keep Reston financed any longer, and its management was taken over by Gulf Oil, there was uneasiness about the future not only of Reston but also of new towns generally. Wolf Von Eckardt, architecture critic of the *Washington Post,* commented soon afterward, Nov. 19, 1967: "Gulf Oil's clumsy putsch in Reston . . . has considerably damaged hopes that large corporations will be able to make a constructive investment in the rebuilding of American cities."

Robert L. Durham, president of the American Institute of Architects, had written in the same newspaper the previous day: "It would be a mistake to believe Reston's current problems raise questions about the viability of the 'new town' movement, or about Reston's design. The project's difficulties . . . reflect the fact that in the United States we have not yet faced up to the special kind of financing needed by new towns."

This year, for the first time, federal housing officials believe they have obtained a workable provision of law offering the kind of assistance that new towns need. The Housing and Urban Development Act of 1968, signed into law Aug. 1 by President Johnson, authorizes the government to guarantee

---

[7] Ada Louise Huxtable, *New York Times,* Sept. 25, 1967.

bonds, notes and other obligations in amounts up to $50 million for a single development. Total federal guarantees are not to exceed $250 million at any one time. Officials in the Department of Housing and Urban Development explained to Editorial Research Reports that with these federal guarantees behind their loans, new town developers would be able to defer repayments in the early years when profits are nil. A law passed two years earlier had contained a provision for mortgage insurance for new communities, but HUD officials said it was virtually unworkable.

Big-city mayors are apprehensive lest new towns compete with the cities for federal funds, and southern congressmen fear that new towns will encourage "race mixing." The mayors' opposition seems to have declined, but many federal officials are aware of a latent hostility in Congress to programs that smack of "social engineering." HUD officials refer to "new communities" but rarely ever speak of "new towns," thinking that the new towns of Europe give the name a socialistic connotation.

European Experience With New Towns

GREAT BRITAIN has made new towns an element of national planning for almost a quarter of a century, and in that time it has become the world's most prolific builder of new towns. Since passage of the New Towns Act of 1946, some 24 communities of this kind have been built or planned under government sponsorship in England, Wales and Scotland. The act provided for the creation of public corporations, appointed and financed by the National Ministry of Town and Country Planning, to build the towns.

The purpose was to drain off excess growth in the big cities, provide needed new housing, and save the remaining countryside from suburban sprawl—or "overspill" as the English say. The British problem is magnified by a present-day average population density of more than 800 persons per square mile in England and Wales, as compared with about 670 in the most heavily populated region of the United States, the Boston-New York-Washington megalopolis.[8]

---

[8] See "Megalopolis: Promise and Problems," *E.R.R.*, 1965 Vol. I, p. 103, and "Population Profile of the United States," *E.R.R.*, 1967 Vol. II, p. 803.

The rationale of British new towns borrows heavily from a concept promoted at the turn of the century by Ebenezer Howard. In his influential book *Tomorrow* (1898), Howard preached that crowded Londoners would become healthier and happier if many of them moved beyond the fringe of the great metropolis into surrounding "garden cities." He viewed London as a classic example of chaotic growth.

Two garden cities inspired by Howard, Letchworth and Welwyn, were built in the early decades of this century. "Both of these communities," Lewis Mumford has said, "starting as private enterprises, with limited prospects of gain, not merely survived indifference and opposition, but have affected the pattern of housing and city-building in many areas, from Scotland to India." [9] But Howard, unlike some of his disciples, did not stop with the concept of a single garden city or a scattering of them. Rather, he envisioned, according to Mumford, "the creation of a regional unit that would bring into a single organized system at least 10 cities with a total population of 300,000, bounded together by a rapid public transportation system. . . ." [10]

Garden cities were to be separated from one another by an expanse of open space or "greenbelt." In England today the term has taken on a fairly precise meaning, a large swath of encircling land that has been placed off-limits to development. It may be a combination of public and private acreage, some of it used for parks and recreation. But the main purpose is to stop "overspill" and to channel urban growth out beyond the greenbelt into new towns.

Since the time of Elizabeth I, who banned all new buildings within three miles of London's gates, the English have habitually viewed the growth of their cities with consternation and sought ways to control it. The Green Belt Act of 1938 authorized the government to begin buying land to form a London greenbelt. Within 30 years it had become a reality, with 840 square miles secured. Meanwhile, in 1955, the government urged other cities to follow the London example.

The outward growth of London has been forced to leapfrog over the greenbelt into encircling new towns. Many of

---

[9] Lewis Mumford, *The City in History* (1961), p. 522.

[10] Lewis Mumford, introduction to Sir Frederic Osborn and Arnold Whittick, *The New Towns: The Answer to Metropolis* (1963), pp. 2-3.

them were built around existing villages and towns. The village fathers agreed to the planned expansion because, often, their region was in need of jobs. New towns guaranteed the arrival of factories—a vital element of new-town planning. Manufacturers are lured to the designated sites by a variety of government incentives. Plants and offices are built with public funds and leased to the companies at low rates, and their workers have first choice of available housing—at rentals as low as $12 a week for a three-bedroom unit.

Availability of housing is an enticement to Londoners living in cramped quarters. The Greater London Council reported recently that the housing shortage could be expected to worsen rather than improve over the years. But Britishers are less inclined than Americans to break family ties and move to another city. For this reason, British housing authorities have gone to unusual lengths—by American standards—to keep family groups together and lessen the disruptive effect of moving into a new town.

NEW TOWNS IN BRITAIN: HOUSING VS. AESTHETICS

The Ministry of Housing and Local Government reported in midsummer that more houses had been completed in Britain during the first half of 1968 than during any comparable period in history. Since 1945, when the last German bomb fell on the British Isles, one family in three has been rehoused. Even so, one house in four is still without such amenities as indoor toilets, bathrooms and running water.

New towns built since the war have provided rehousing for 800,000 Britons, 250,000 of them from London. Yet, housing shortage or no, all do not find new towns their cup of tea. Complaints appear frequently in the press. *Daily Telegraph* writer Andrew Alexander recently characterized new towns as "neither large enough to provide attractive facilities nor small enough to be friendly communities." His article of Aug. 15, 1968, set off a spate of letters to the editor. One man wrote that he had lived in a new town for 11 years and "found it almost unendurable." He said that "The depressing architecture . . . makes one sorry for children growing up in such ugly places." Others wrote that the people who live there are young and bored—complaints that might well have come from American suburbs.

The same parallel is found in literature. British writer Angus Wilson set his novel *Late Call* (1963) in an English new town, which he depicted as no more of a utopia than an American suburb. The Ministry of Housing and Local Government said in its 1960 annual report that the malady known as "new-town blues" had been greatly exaggerated in some press articles, but it acknowledged that it undoubtedly existed: "Social workers and doctors have long recognized it as one of the difficulties . . . which perhaps only time can overcome." Frank Schaffer, Secretary of the Commission for New Towns, wrote to the *Daily Telegraph* that the towns could have been built better except for credit squeezes in the 1950s and 1960s. When faced with a choice, the planners gave housing priority over aesthetic values.

Architects have acclaimed the new town of Cambernauld in Scotland as a striking departure from the blandness of most British new towns. The American Institute of Architects in 1967 awarded the planners and architects of Cambernauld the first R. S. Reynolds Memorial Award, a $25,000 scholarship fund for training in community architecture.

SCANDINAVIAN SUCCESS WITH SATELLITE CITIES

From an architectural point of view, Scandinavian new towns are the most admired in Europe. Farsta and Vallingby near Stockholm, and Tapiola near Helsinki, are lauded for beauty and excellent design. Speaking of the first two, Wolf Von Eckardt has said: "These Swedish communities with their well-kept parks, gardens, and abundant playgrounds and their strict separation of cars and pedestrians, make even the best of our suburbs look woefully deprived." But he added that most of the people lived in fairly uniform high-rise apartment buildings, and "I never quite lost an awareness of the benign workings of a welfare state." In contrast, Von Eckardt observed, "Tapiola looks and feels as spontaneously lusty and natural in an endearingly well-behaved sort of way as the Finnish children that swarm all over." [11]

Heikki von Hertzen, the Tapiola builder, is quoted as saying that prosperity came slowly to Finland because the country had to pay exorbitant war reparations to Russia. "As we finally began to catch up with the West, we asked ourselves: 'What are we to do with our new affluence? We can't eat more. There is a limit to the automobiles and gadgets we

---

[11] Wolf Von Eckardt, *A Place to Live* (1967), pp. 350-351.

really need.' So I started to persuade my countrymen that we should build a suitable and beautiful environment for everyone." [12]

Von Hertzen did his persuading with Finnish labor unions, the Family Welfare League, several women's clubs and other citizen groups. They founded a non-profit housing foundation, obtained bank loans, bought the land and went to work. The foundation has since begun to build several similar new towns throughout Finland in accordance with a national plan that is intended to keep "urban sprawl" away from the environs of Helsinki and prevent the capital, which is situated on a peninsula surrounded by islands, from becoming an overgrown metropolitan area.

Reston has often been compared to Tapiola in beauty. There are also other similarities—both are being built by private enterprise and both are having difficulty providing low-income housing. So far, the American model of new-town building has been closer to that of Finland than of any other country in Europe. The new towns of Sweden and several other European countries are built under government sponsorship. In Communist countries like Russia and Yugoslavia, new-town activity is entirely under government control. Even in France, the government is taking the lead in drawing plans for eight new satellite towns to be built within 40 miles of Paris by the end of the century.

The extent to which new-town planning is worldwide becomes apparent from a look at the activity of a single city planning firm, that of Constantinos A. Doxiadis. Doxiadis, sometimes described as the "father of city planners," maintains offices on five continents and a school in his native Athens for teaching what he calls the new science of Ekistics, the study of human settlements.[13] His assistants currently are at work preparing new towns in Ghana, Greece, Libya and Pakistan.

DIFFERENCES IN AMERICAN AND BRITISH APPROACH

In delivering the Godkin Lectures at Harvard in March 1965, Robert C. Weaver indicated that he found little in the English example of new-town building that could be trans-

---

[12] *Ibid.*, p. 351.

[13] Historians say the ancient Greek city-states maintained a policy of building new towns when the old ones reached a population of about 30,000. The ancient Egyptians and Romans were also builders of new towns.

planted to America. He pointed to differences in tradition and instruments of government between the two countries that colored their approach to new towns. The British system entails public ownership of new-town lands, which are leased to tenants. This practice, Weaver noted, is facilitated by an array of English precedents lacking in this country. Since the days of feudalism, aristocratic landowners in England have permitted tenants to occupy their estates under various arrangements. But in America since its earliest days there has been strong feeling for individual private ownership— the antithesis of the English leasehold system.

Moreover, there is little consensus in the United States about the desirability of reducing the population of the country's large cities. "Rather we have great concern for preserving and expanding the tax base of our central cities," Weaver said. ". . . Whatever the primary role of new communities may be in this nation, it is certainly not to accomplish the stated objectives of the British new towns."

Weaver predicted, correctly so far, that the new communities in this country would be conceived and constructed by private enterprise—places more akin to Park Forest in Illinois than to the government-sponsored Greenbelt towns of the New Deal era. Park Forest, 30 miles from Chicago, was the first American new community started and finished during the period immediately after World War II. It offered novel and advanced patterns of urban living, including cluster development to preserve open space, but it did not aspire to become a self-contained city.[14]

The Greenbelt towns [15] of the Depression Thirties were the first publicly aided garden cities in the Ebenezer Howard tradition to be built in the United States. During World War II and afterward, the federal government created the "atomic cities" of Los Alamos, N.M.; Hanford, Wash., and Oak Ridge, Tenn. But this was an act of military rather than social concern.

---

[14] The middle-class way of life in Park Forest is described in great detail by William H. Whyte in *The Organization Man* (1956).

[15] Greenbelt, Md.; Greendale, Wis., and Greenhills, Ohio, built by the Resettlement Administration of the Agriculture Department. See Albert Mayer, "Greenbelt Towns Revisited," *Journal of Housing*, January 1967, pp. 12-26, and "City Beautiful," *E.R.R.*, 1964 Vol. I, p. 163.

Planning for the Cities of the Future

AMERICAN PLANNERS of new towns or cities belong to one or the other of two schools of thought. One school would build new cities on the fringes of metropolitan areas, separate from the inner city but sharing in its economic and social life. The other school would build new cities in underpopulated expanses of the country, far from existing big cities. The "dispersal" advocates point out that already 70 per cent of the people of the United States live on less than 2 per cent of the land area.

Each school can point to a working of natural forces in its favor. The physical specifications for new cities virtually dictate that planners look beyond the metropolitan areas to large virgin sites. Besides the problem of land acquisition, new cities encounter a tangle of overlapping governmental jurisdictions in metropolitan areas.[16] Hackensack Meadows, a boggy expanse of New Jersey only five miles from mid-Manhattan, has been suggested often as a new-town site. But it has been pointed out also that a developer would have to negotiate with 18 local governments—a formidable obstacle in itself.

On the other hand, existing big cities exercise a strong gravitational pull. New towns placed in the hinterlands might be doomed to failure. An exponent of that philosophy is Constantinos Doxiadis, the city planning theorist. He tours the world explaining his concept of building "smallness within size"—clusters of individual communities forming the city as a whole.

The "dispersal" men think that in time a redistribution of the population will become inevitable, and they wish to prepare for that day in an orderly way. Urban critic Lewis Mumford holds little hope that existing American cities can long survive present conditions. "I wouldn't give the American city 50 years," he told a network television interviewer. "I . . . foresee disaster much earlier than that."[17]

Secretary of Agriculture Orville L. Freeman recently

---

[16] See "Local Government Modernization," *E.R.R.*, 1967 Vol. II, p. 739.

[17] Columbia Broadcasting System special program "To Build the Future," June 26, 1968.

advocated a national policy of creating new cities in the distant countryside—on sites selected by his department. Freeman suggested, as a start, 25 to 50 new cities built 100 miles or more apart, but linked by high-speed transit. Referring to Reston and Columbia, he said: "It will take more than a few builders with vision to prepare for 100 million people in the time that is left in this century." [18]

'EXPERIMENTAL CITY' AND 'SYSTEMS ENGINEERING'

While Freeman's thinking is only at the trial-balloon stage, that of Athelstan Spilhaus has reached the drawing board. Spilhaus heads a team of urban thinkers who are creating the blueprint "Experimental City," a laboratory for urban living of the future which may someday rise in Freeman's home state of Minnesota or in a neighboring state. The project was conceived while Spilhaus was professor of physics at the University of Minnesota; he is now president of the Franklin Institute in Philadelphia.

The Spilhaus planners envision a city of 250,000, built from scratch, to test the value of "systems engineering" and of some far-out products and designs in urban life. Spilhaus explained that "housing units may be precast, even prefabricated . . . with units put together like building blocks, and arranged and rearranged." [19] A geodesic dome two miles in diameter would cover a part of the city for climate and health control. Waste water would be purified and reused; a futuristic mass transit system would carry passengers free of charge.

To complete the initial planning phase this year, Spilhaus won financial backing from 10 private concerns and three federal agencies. The departments of Commerce, Housing and Urban Development, and Health, Education and Welfare together made $248,000 available for the study. Site selection and actual building remain in the future. The planners' time-table calls for completion some 20 to 30 years hence.

Spilhaus hopes to demonstrate, among other things, that if the 200 million people now living in the United States were grouped in 800 cities of a quarter of a million people each, there would be an absence of pollution, traffic congestion, riots and many other urban ills.

---

[18] Speech before Georgia County Commissioners Association, Augusta, April 30, 1968.
[19] Athelstan Spilhaus, "The Experimental City," *Science*, Feb. 16, 1968, p. 711.

"Systems engineering" in city building is still in its infancy. The phrase, *Fortune* writer Lawrence Lessing has explained, is at its simplest just logical common-sense planning. "At its most sophisticated, it is an uncommon, intricately organized method for bringing to bear all relevant scientific, technical and other sources upon the analysis and subsequent solution of complex problems." Lessing added:

> Many systems men . . . believe that systems engineering can show what it really can do for urban problems only when it takes on the building of entirely new cities, completely outside the old ones. . . .
> The nearest thing to a systems approach to a new city is Columbia, Maryland. . . . To start with, a hypothetical economic model was set up, detailing all the land, structures, and utilities needed for a complete city of that size, and projecting its cost and the businesses and industries needed to sustain it.[20]

But Columbia represents a limited-scale application of the systems approach because it has not drawn upon technological innovation. It does not make use of potential new materials, building techniques and systems, which cannot be used in code-restricted cities but which might be pioneered elsewhere to realize dramatically reduced building costs.

Bernard A. Schriever, a member of the planning board of "Experimental City," is in the process of organizing a consortium of 10 or more leading aerospace, electronics, construction and architectural engineering companies to employ "systems engineering" in a broad-scale attack on the problems involved in making cities more workable. Schriever, a retired general, once directed the Air Force missile program.

BUILDING OF NEW CITIES FOR NATIONAL CAPITALS

Another member of the "Experimental City" planning board is the inventor-designer, Buckminster Fuller. In his lectures and writings, Fuller has said that industry of the future will be placed outside the cities and will be largely automated. He theorizes that the cities will increasingly become places for the exchange of what he calls "metaphysical values"—ideas, learning and culture—rather than physical goods. By that reasoning, cities need no longer be built by a sea, a river, or a coal field; they can be placed anywhere that technology permits.

Brazil built its new capital of Brasilia in the country's vast interior on a site so remote that all supplies had to be

[20] Lawrence Lessing, "Systems Engineering Invades the City," *Fortune*, January 1968, pp. 156, 220.

flown in. Doxiadis contends that, except for new capitals, most new cities are being built on too small a scale. In an article written for the 1968 Britannica *Book of the Year,* he cited Brasilia, Islamabad and Chandigarh as notable exceptions. Islamabad is the new capital of Pakistan and Chandigarh the new capital of the Indian state of Punjab.

Pakistan had to meet the need for an administrative capital when it gained independence in 1947. It first used Karachi, a provincial town with few of the facilities required by the capital of a nation of 90 million people. A study proved that it would be cheaper to build a new capital elsewhere than to try to rebuild Karachi. An area near the existing city of Rawalpindi was selected, because it had rail and road connections and an airport. "In this way," Doxiadis said, "the birth and growth of the new city imitated the biological process of birth and growth. Rawalpindi acted as the mother, feeding the child until, one day, it grows enough to act as its mother's protector." Islamabad is conceived as a growing area that someday will embrace Rawalpindi.

Older capitals built from scratch include Washington, D. C., and Canberra, Australia. All have been based on the industry of government. Significantly, this practice runs counter to the belief of planners that new towns should offer a wide spectrum of jobs, attracting people from all levels of education, income and skills. No new town yet fulfills these aims. Some of the British new towns are factory-worker communities and provide a number of jobs, but the range is narrow.

AID OF NEW TOWNS IN SOLVING GHETTO PROBLEM

New-town defenders say that the shortage of jobs in new towns may fairly be criticized in Britain where there are stated national goals for these communities. But in America perhaps more social benefits are expected of new towns than their private developers ever set out to attain. The very existence of new towns has raised hopes that they may become, to some extent, a refuge for persons trying to get away from the ills of the inner city. Joseph P. Lyford, in a study of slum problems in New York City a few years ago, said: "The airtight cage of poverty, frustration, and fear in which the people of the city are imprisoned can be broken open and new towns founded. . . ." He added that unless new communities were founded, it was "difficult to see how the poor, especially the Negro, can ever become truly integrated into American life." Because the suburban ring around New York City has "locked the Negro into the slum," new settlements would have to "leap over this constricting belt."[21] Lyford proposed that New York City buy land for satellite towns far beyond its boundaries.

However, New York City is in chronic financial trouble, and it cannot be expected to finance satellite cities—even if it were legally authorized to do so. William L. Slayton, executive vice president of Urban America, advocates the creation of a federally aided public development corporation to build new cities. Slayton, former administrator of federal urban renewal programs, has proposed that such corporations be chartered by the states and empowered to purchase land and plan its use with the assistance of long-term federal loans. The corporations would then sell or lease the land to private concerns in accordance with the city plan. Slayton said the new communities "cannot simply be new spas for exurbanites." He insisted that "They must provide an alternative to decaying city cores as places of residence for the poor, especially the Negro poor. . . ."[22]

PLACE OF NEW TOWNS IN FUTURE SUBURBAN GROWTH

Others view the potentialities of new towns in terms less of alleviating inner-city problems than of protecting the outlying countryside from despoliation. Dennis O'Harrow, executive director of the American Society of Planning Officials, affirms that large-scale developments are inevitable and "if they are not to be sprawl, they must be reasonably self-sufficient and self-contained."[23] Herbert J. Gans, a sociologist who has written about suburbia at length, reports that another huge wave of suburban home-building can be expected in the coming decade. The first children born of the 1947-1960 "baby boom" are now beginning to marry and produce families of their own. "Only simple addition is necessary to see that by the mid-seventies, they will be fashioning another massive suburban building boom."[24]

Gans said studies of housing preference indicate that the majority of Americans, including those now living in the

---

[21] Joseph P. Lyford, *The Airtight Cage* (book developed from a study prepared for the Center for the Study of Democratic Institutions, 1966), pp. 341-342.

[22] Speech before American Society of Planning Officials, Houston, Texas, April 4, 1967.

[23] Dennis O'Harrow, "New Towns or New Sprawl?" *ASPO Newsletter*, October 1964.

[24] Herbert J. Gans, "The White Exodus to Suburbia Steps Up," *New York Times Magazine*, Jan. 7, 1968, p. 25.

city, want a suburban single-family house once they have children, and want to remain in that house until their children grow up. He said Reston's slow start suggested that "exquisitely designed communal recreational areas cannot substitute for private space. Most home buyers do not want that much togetherness."

But William H. Whyte regards cluster development, such as Reston employs, as the coming trend. "The move to high-density centers not only makes for a much better land use; it happens to be more economic for the commercial interests involved." Whyte has predicted a filling-in of the bypassed land in the gray areas between city and suburbia, and a more intensive development—or redevelopment—of suburbia itself. There will be new towns, he says, "but I will wager that the ones which work out will not be self-contained and that they will not be off somewhere in the hinterland. We are, in sum, going to operate metropolitan areas much closer to capacity and with more people living on a given amount of land." [25]

There is a tendency to look for a single solution to all urban problems. For those who regard new towns as that solution, only disappointment is likely in the foreseeable future. But where the aims of the well-wishers are more modest, there is hope of partial fulfillment. At the least, new towns may influence the suburbs of tomorrow in the right direction. Already there is evidence that new towns have inspired—or forced—conventional developers to elevate their standards of design and land usage.

---

[25] William H. Whyte, *The Last Landscape* (1968), p. 8.

▼▼▼